GOSPEL
REVOLUTION

ALLOWING GOD TO AWAKEN OUR PASSION FOR THE GOSPEL

Endorsements

Paul gave it straight to Timothy: ". . . Christ Jesus came into the world to save sinners." But sometimes in our rush as Christ-followers to turn sinners into believers we have played to their felt needs more than their real need. Humanity is not merely broken; it is spiritually dead and only the regenerating power of God the Spirit can bring new life. And how has He chosen to do that? Through the gospel message that begins in Genesis and is threaded throughout the biblical story. The gospel is God at His best, and *Gospel Revolution* describes and defends it accurately, biblically, powerfully, and, most of all, in an approachable manner. Gabriel Garcia writes what he has known personally and taught professionally, and has given the church a powerful tool for learning and for training our people to "live as lights in the world, holding forth the Word of life." Read it and then read it again.

> Dr. David W. Hegg, Senior Pastor, Grace Baptist Church,
> Santa Clarita, California; author of *The Obedience Option*

The gospel of Jesus Christ is not just the ABC's of the Christian life. is the A-to-Z of the Christian life. The gospel is *the* engine that propels, motivates, and energizes the Christian life. Nothing is more foundational to the Christian life than an on-going preaching of the gospel to the inner recesses of our souls. In *Gospel Revolution*, Gabriel Garcia has written a wonderful resource to point the Christian towards daily gospel application. Anyone who has tried religion and found themselves wanting will find in this book the key to unlock the kind of life that Jesus promises.

> Peter Hong, Lead Pastor, New Community Covenant Church
> (Logan Square), Chicago, Illinois; Director of NC3 Church Planting

I have discovered few books that so clearly, potently, and methodically lay truth before me like a feast as this book has. It has served as a catapult for my soul, taking it to new heights. What makes the book impacting is knowing the character of its author. Gabe's life provides a rich context for the book and validates the truth contained in its pages. He walks his talk. I would implore the digesting of this book not only for your own soul, but for the nations that God has commanded us to reach and disciple. This book will serve as an intimate companion of mine for years to come.

> Gary Gaddini, Lead Pastor, Peninsula Covenant Church,
> Redwood City, California

GOSPEL
REVOLUTION

ALLOWING GOD TO AWAKEN OUR PASSION FOR THE GOSPEL

GABRIEL GARCIA

A Devotional: with Study Guide

Gospel Revolution

ISBN: 978-1-936907-03-8

Published by HOME IMPROVEMENT MINISTRIES.
For information on other H.I.M. resources, please contact:
   HOME IMPROVEMENT MINISTRIES
   213 Burlington Road, Suite 101-B
   Bedford, MA 01730
E-mail inquiries: info@HIMweb.org
Website: www.HIMweb.org

Acknowledgments

I'd like to thank my amazing and beautiful wife, Kari, for always supporting, loving, and believing in me. I love doing life, ministry, and now raising a family with you. God could not have blessed me with a more amazing partner in the gospel.

I have to give a huge shout-out to my brother Greg: you have always been there for me and prayed for me, and are continually pushing me towards a Christ-centered life.

My best friend, Ryan Gillespie: thank you for pointing me to Jesus, even when I wasn't interested. You are a better friend than I deserve and a true gift from the Lord.

Thanks to my parents Dan and Debbie Garcia, who have served and loved me in more ways than I will ever be able to comprehend.

To my amazing in-laws, Paul and Virginia Friesen, thank you most of all for letting me marry your daughter, but also for being such a great example of a ministry couple for Kari and me.

To Phil Somerville, thanks for your feedback. To Guy and Barbara Steele, thank you for your meticulous edits and your faithfulness in the assistance of completing this project.

To Alton, Sam, Nay Nay, D-Money, Lee Lee, Lamar, and Jessica, I pray that you continue to live gospel-centered lives for the glory of God.

Most importantly, I want to thank Jesus Christ for coming into this world to live and die as my Savior. I obviously don't deserve Your grace and a relationship with You but I hope to live a life of faithfulness in response to what You have done for me and others.

Contents

SECTION FOUR: A Faithful Response to the Gospel

SECTION FIVE: Advancing the Gospel

STUDY GUIDE

This book is dedicated to my son Brandon.
May God grow you to be a man who knows, loves,
and gives his life away for the gospel.

Introduction

The gospel should revolutionize our lives; in fact, it is only the gospel that can bring a total life transformation, provide us with forgiveness of sins, and, most importantly, reconcile us to God.

For many Christians today, the gospel often becomes stale, dry and lifeless. For many years of my life, the gospel tasted like those wafers we get when we take communion once a month. We eat the wafer, but everybody knows it doesn't taste good. In the same way, I learned how to endure the gospel but not enjoy the gospel. I knew the gospel, but I didn't receive life from the gospel. I was mildly thankful for the gospel, but I did not eternally cherish and rejoice in the gospel. As a result, the gospel wasn't having the life-changing impact on my life that it was meant to have. I was failing to live a God-honoring life in light of who Christ is and what He accomplished on my behalf.

Hopefully, through the *Gospel Revolution*, God will bring you to a deep understanding of and a passionate joy for the central focus of the scriptures, which tell us that:

- We are in need of a Savior because we have all rebelled against God.
- In love, God sent His perfect and sinless Son, Jesus Christ, to the cross to die for our sins and to rescue us from the punishment we deserve.
- Jesus Christ rose from the dead three days later, solidifying His work on the cross as the saving act that forgives sins and reconciles us to God through repentance and faith.

Our goal as Christians should be to fall in love with the gospel and never wander from the revolutionary truth of what Christ has done to bring us into a restored relationship with God through His perfect life, death on the cross, and resurrection.

The simple but revolutionary message of the gospel can be seen in what Paul writes to the Ephesians:

But God, being rich in mercy, because of the great love with which he loved us, even when we were dead in our trespasses, made us alive together with Christ—by grace you have been saved—and raised us up with him and seated us with him in the heavenly places in Christ Jesus, so that in the coming ages he might show the immeasurable riches of his grace in kindness toward us in Christ Jesus. For by grace you have been saved through faith. And this is not your own doing; it is the gift of God, not a result of works, so that no one may boast. (Ephesians 2:4–9)

The *Gospel Revolution* is not a new scheme or gimmick that promises wealth or a pain-free life. However, it is a reminder of the eternal truths that we unfortunately drift away from. The aim of this book is that we come to a deeper knowledge of the gospel while allowing God to awaken our hearts to lifelong passion for the gospel. The fruit of this God-led endeavor will hopefully bring us to a place of cherishing our restored relationship with God while opening our eyes to how the gospel impacts every aspect of our lives.

Too often, we as Christians act as if the gospel were something that we graduate from; quite the contrary, the more we mature, the more we will realize that we should never abandon or turn our back on the splendid truths of the gospel. As we allow God to ignite a revolution in our lives through the gospel, He will lead us to an abundant life that is primarily concerned with living a life of worship in response to the great gift of the gospel.

If the gospel is not completely central to one's life, it will be impossible to fully bring glory to God or to gain true spiritual maturity, eternal significance, or earthly joy. If milk does a body good, the gospel is what will make us spiritually healthy, strong and mature. Without Christ and His work on the cross as the focal point of our lives, we will begin to spiritually decay, and our churches will lose the authority and power they have been entrusted with by God.

One of the reasons we fail to experience a life of great intimacy with God, continual spiritual growth, and joy, peace, and purpose is that we've become so focused on ourselves. We are focused on finding *our* joy, *our* contentment, and meaning for *our* lives. But despite our best efforts, we can't seem to find the so-called "better life" we are looking for. The problem is that we have made life about ourselves when life is really about God. As we allow God to transform us through the gospel, we will become less and less concerned about ourselves and more and more concerned about honoring and glorifying God in all we do. Through this transformation we will actually experience the fullness of life that Christ has come to give us.

No matter who you are, the message of the gospel is relevant, life-changing, and powerful each and every day of our lives. However, if you want to experience the full power of the gospel, you must continually saturate yourself with its truth and respond to it with faithfulness. God's desire is to have the gospel at the center of what we think, what we do, and who we are. C. J. Mahaney writes, "If there's anything in life we should be passionate about, it's the gospel. And I don't mean passionate only about sharing it with others; I mean passionate in thinking about the gospel, reflecting upon it, rejoicing in it, allowing it to color the way we look at the world and all of life."

So what is the *Gospel Revolution*? It is the journey that God wants to take us on so that the gospel never becomes anything less than the defining truth and greatest joy of our lives. When the gospel is biblically understood, appropriately digested, and forever cherished, it can have no other impact than a complete revolution and transformation of our lives.

Honestly, does the gospel impact every day of your life and every aspect of who you are? Do you know how to let the message of the gospel permeate your thoughts, guide your actions and radically alter your life? This book is about exploring the never-ending nuances and implications of the gospel and letting its life-changing message alter every aspect of who you are and who you are becoming.

If you are not sure you believe the gospel message, I pray that you slowly and contemplatively work through each chapter and each scripture and allow God to point you to Jesus Christ and the good news of the gospel. Be open to the possibility that it could be true. I wholeheartedly believe that the gospel has the power to change your life and that God, through His grace, will meet your needs and give you hope, purpose, and an unexplainable peace. However, the most staggering blessing that we receive when we place our faith in Christ is that we begin to have an authentic relationship with God. My prayer is that you will see that Jesus is worthy of your full devotion and that you will make the greatest decision of your life—the decision to place your faith in the saving work of Christ.

To my Christian brothers and sisters, I hope that God uses this book to reawaken a strong passion in your heart for what Christ has done for us on the cross. God desires that the gospel be the center of your life and that everything else will spring forth from God's amazing grace, especially the passion and joy of knowing and pleasing Him.

Though I am forever grateful for the journey that God has brought me on, I know that I am not there yet. A deeper understanding of the gospel will be a lifelong endeavor, never fully arriving, but continually moving towards a fuller picture of God's love shown through what Christ has done to serve us by going to the cross.

This is the *Gospel Revolution*, that by God's grace our lives will never be the same, as we understand, meditate on, and fall in love with the good news of Jesus Christ, seeking to bring Him glory in all we do.

Section One

The God of the Gospel

The gospel starts and ends with God.
And to our benefit, the gospel is the beautiful canvas on
which God's characteristics are clearly on display.

Psalm 96:1–6

Oh sing to the LORD a new song;
sing to the LORD, all the earth!
Sing to the LORD, bless his name;
tell of his salvation from day to day.
Declare his glory among the nations,
his marvelous works among all the peoples!
For great is the LORD, and greatly to be praised;
he is to be feared above all gods.
For all the gods of the peoples are worthless idols,
but the LORD made the heavens.
Splendor and majesty are before him;
strength and beauty are in his sanctuary.

1

Created for Relationship

Genesis 1:26–27

Then God said, "Let us make man in our image, after our likeness. And let them have dominion over the fish of the sea and over the birds of the heavens and over the livestock and over all the earth and over every creeping thing that creeps on the earth." So God created man in his own image, in the image of God he created him; male and female he created them.

As we examine the early chapters of Genesis, to our delight, we see that we were created to be in a relationship with God. God does more than just offer to be in a relationship with us; He deeply wants to be in a perfect relationship with us. I guess we can't fully imagine what a perfect relationship with God would look like, because we've never been able to experience a perfect relationship with anyone. However, God created us to have this kind of relationship with Him; it is what God desires for us.

Implicit in these early chapters of Genesis is that God created us to be in a loving, deep and joyful relationship with Him. Adam and Eve built and sustained that relationship through their commitment to glorify God by obeying all His commands. In the first two chapters of Genesis, we get a glimpse of the way this world was supposed to be. At the center of that world was man uninhibited in building a thriving relationship with God through a commitment to honoring and enjoying God above all else.

It is in the third chapter of Genesis that we see the fall of man when Adam and Eve sin against God. From that point on, sin corrupts humanity and blocks our ability to be perfectly united to God. As Adam and Eve begin to recognize the shame of their disobedience, we get a glimpse of how our relationship with God was forever changed.

> *And they heard the sound of the Lord God walking in the garden in the cool of the day, and the man and his wife hid themselves from the presence of the Lord God among the trees of the garden.* (Genesis 3:8)

Because of the shame that had overtaken them, Adam and Eve ran and hid from God's presence in the Garden. From this point on, all of humanity, including you and I, have been actively sinning and running from God. No matter how good we think we are, at some point in our lives, we have all been passionately committed to avoiding God's commandments. As a result, we have run from Him and missed out on the greatest relationship possible.

Is there a relationship more refreshing, nourishing and loving than a relationship with our Creator, the Creator of the heavens and earth? Throughout the scriptures we see God jumping off the pages, saying, "I want to be your God and I want you to be my people." Our God is a relational God and, amazingly, He wants to be in a relationship with us. Despite our constant disobedience, we see throughout the Bible that God is determined to provide a way to reconcile us, sinners that we are, to Him, a holy God. If it were us, we would give up on people after they have hurt us over and over again. Yet, we have a God who is willing to reconcile us to Him, despite what we have done to Him. This is the revolutionary news of the gospel.

The gospel starts with our problem of sin. Sin can only be fixed through Jesus Christ and it is only through the mediation of Jesus that we can begin to rebuild what once existed in the Garden. Paul writes in the New Testament that we have a God *"who desires all people to be saved and to come to the knowledge of the truth. For there is one God, and there is one mediator between God and men, the man Christ Jesus, who gave himself as a ransom for all"*

(1 Timothy 2:4–6). Though we are lovers of sin, God proves that He is committed to providing a way for us to reconstruct our broken relationship with Him.

We can rejoice in the truth that, despite our continual disobedience, God wants to know us and grow with us. God wants to be our God and He wants us to be His people. When we turn to Revelation, the last book of the Bible, it shows us what will happen when we are reconciled to God. *"Behold, the dwelling place of God is with man. He will dwell with them, and they will be his people, and God himself will be with them as their God"* (Revelation 21:3).

The gospel is our road back to the Garden. Through Christ, we can look forward to the day when all things will be made right and we will be with God and God will be with us. We will experience God just as Adam and Eve were able to in the Garden of Eden. Only through Christ can we start building that relationship with God today; a relationship we are created for; a relationship God desires.

Make It Personal

1. We see that sin has broken our relationship with God and created a huge problem. Does God have to fix our problem?

2. God desires a relationship with you. How does that make you feel? Do you share that desire? If you share that desire, how does it show in your life?

3. If God wants to know you more intimately, what can you do to invest more fully in your relationship with Him?

Scriptures to Read

1. Genesis 1–3

2. Revelation 21

A Moment of Prayer

- Pray that God will help you understand more fully His desire to know you.

- Pray that God will show you and others that it is only through Christ that we can be reconciled to God.

- Pray that the Spirit would lead you to a deeper and more intimate relationship with your Creator.

The Holiness of God

Isaiah 6:1-3

In the year that King Uzziah died I saw the Lord sitting upon a throne, high and lifted up; and the train of his robe filled the temple. Above him stood the seraphim. Each had six wings; with two he covered his face, and with two he covered his feet, and with two he flew. And one called to another and said: "Holy, holy, holy is the Lord of hosts; the whole earth is full of his glory!"

Through the vision of the prophet Isaiah, we see one of the most staggering characteristics of our God: His holiness. The word "holy" means "to be set apart." It is God, and God alone, who is set apart in perfect holiness. It is our God who sits upon a throne, lifted up, with angelic beings praising His holiness.

What comes to mind when you think of holiness? For me, images of old ladies come to mind; ones who are extremely sweet, seem to pray all day long, and are always willing to bake you something. When others think of holiness they think of people like Mother Teresa or Billy Graham. Usually, when we think of holiness, we think of people who are really, really, *really* good.

For God, to be holy means something far more than just being "really good." God *is* holiness. Unlike us, God doesn't need to run from sin. God doesn't need to program Himself to be holy. He doesn't need to work on being really, really good. God has been, and always will be, fully set apart. A.W. Tozer writes, "Holy is the way God is. To be holy He does not conform to a standard. He is that standard. He is absolutely holy with an infinite, incomprehensive fullness of purity that is incapable of being other than it is." God is perfectly righteous, perfectly pure, and perfectly, well, perfect. God stands apart. His holiness never wavers and is never compromised. God will never stop being completely holy in all He is and all He does.

While God reflects holiness, we know that we are people plagued by a sinful nature. This is a problem. Because of His holiness, God must condemn us based on our flawed character. Reflecting on God's holiness, the prophet Habakkuk says that God's *"eyes are too pure to look on evil; (He) cannot tolerate wrong"* (Habakkuk 1:13, NIV).

Ever since sin entered God's perfect creation, God has been looking forward to, and planning, a day when wickedness will be fully crushed from existence and holiness fully restored in the new heavens and new earth. In God's perfect plan, the sins of the world were laid upon the sacrificial lamb of Jesus Christ. God punished Christ as if He were punishing the sins of those who put their faith in Him. As a result, instead of being alienated from God because of our unholiness, we are reconciled to God because of the holiness of Jesus.

But now, through faith in Christ and the empowerment of the Holy Spirit, we can start to shed our old life of sin and begin to live a new life marked by holiness. For us, to be holy is to run from sin and run towards the righteous life that we have been called to live; a life modeled to us by Jesus Christ. The apostle Peter writes, *"As obedient children, do not be conformed to the passions of your former ignorance, but as he who called you is holy, you also be holy in all your conduct, since it is written, 'You shall be holy, for I am holy'"* (1 Peter 1:14–16). A life of holiness doesn't come easy. We have to pursue holiness, fight for holiness, and depend on God for holiness.

However, even as we put forth our best efforts towards living a holy life, we are still people who struggle against sin. Perhaps it's our daily struggle with sin that serves as a visible reminder of the difference between us and God. God's holiness should continually reveal to us our sin while bringing us to a place of awe, reverence, and even fear towards Him. The psalmist writes, *"Ascribe to the LORD the glory due his name; worship the LORD in the splendor of holiness"* (Psalm 29:2).

There will come a day, when Christ returns, when God will restore His creation for all of eternity to complete holiness. But even now, as we anticipate that day, we can participate with the angels in praising our holy God as we shout: "Holy, holy, holy is the Lord of hosts."

Make It Personal

1. What does God's holiness reveal to us about His character and our character?

2. In the light of God's holiness, what makes the gospel good news?

3. What can you do to live a life of holiness and reflect the nature of God?

Scriptures to Read

1. Isaiah 6

2. Psalms 29

3. Hebrews 7

A Moment of Prayer

- Pray that God would reveal to you more fully His passion for holiness.

- Pray that God would reveal to you the places in your life that are contrary to God's desire for holiness.

- Pray that God would empower you to take steps towards living a passionate life of holiness.

A Jealous God

Deuteronomy 4:23-24

Take care, lest you forget the covenant of the LORD your God, which he made with you, and make a carved image, the form of anything that the LORD your God has forbidden you. For the LORD your God is a consuming fire, a jealous God.

We often reflect on the love of God, the forgiveness of God, and the compassion of God, but rarely do we reflect on what Moses teaches here: that our *"God is a consuming fire, a jealous God."*

As we continue to build a biblical view of God, we must include the jealousy of God, which is accompanied with anger and can possibly lead to our judgment and condemnation. God is absolutely jealous about anything that replaces Him as our greatest joy or highest treasure, or anything that would knock Him off the throne as the number one priority in our life.

The nation of Israel continually struggled with this sort of rebellion against God. They kept turning towards false gods to replace the one true and living God. Speaking to Moses, God said of the nation of Israel, *"They have turned aside quickly out of the way that I commanded them. They have made for themselves a golden calf and have worshiped it and sacrificed to it"* (Exodus 32:8).

You probably don't worship statues or images. However, if we were to examine our lives, we would probably notice things that are way too important and valuable to us. When I was a child, my parents threatened to take down all the mirrors in the house because every time they saw me I was checking out how good I *thought* I looked. It may be possible that I had a problem with vanity. Instead of being consumed with God, I was consumed with myself.

What are you consumed with? What "carved image" has knocked God off as the greatest joy, highest treasure, and number one priority in your life? Oftentimes, the false gods in our lives have to do with us, *our* status, *our* relationships, *our* finances; anything that promotes self. It is easy to admit that we can be self-centered people and it is often that self-centeredness that creates and elevates false gods in our lives. When we promote self we fail at the greatest responsibility we have in this life—to promote God.

Reflecting on this Old Testament passage from Deuteronomy 4, we must recognize that God will not settle for being anything less than the complete focus of our lives. God is jealous because He *deserves* a total life commitment from us. The first of God's Ten Commandments highlights God's strong desire to be the greatest focus of our lives. God simply but powerfully communicates, *"You shall have no other gods before me"* (Exodus 20:3). In the New Testament, the apostle John writes with similar clarity, *"Little children, keep yourselves from idols"* (1 John 5:21).

As we learn about the jealousy of God, we should be encouraged, because God's jealousy is an indication of how much He truly loves His children. If God weren't jealous of our unfaithfulness, He would not be a God worth following. His lack of jealousy would show that He wasn't concerned about being in a relationship with us. But His jealousy isn't all about us; it is more about Him, and His worth, and what He deserves.

So, as we learn about the jealousy of God, we should be warned. God is not playing around. God will not accept being sent to the sidelines of our lives for the impotent and lifeless idols of this world. If we do not choose to turn from the false gods of this world and place our faith in the saving work of Christ, then we will not experience the blessings that come with the good news of the gospel. The apostle John wrote, *"For God did not send his Son into the world to condemn the world, but in order that the world might be saved through him. Whoever believes in him is not condemned, but whoever does not believe is condemned already, because he has not believed in the name of the only Son of God"* (John 3:17–18).

In response to the saving work of Jesus Christ, we must recognize that God demands and desires our complete devotion to Him. We serve a jealous God who doesn't want to compete with other desires, things, or people in our life. In repentance, we must choose to turn away from any false "god" and seek to know and serve the one and only God. When we do repent and place our faith in Christ, the great news of the gospel is that God will forgive our past unfaithfulness to Him.

Make It Personal

1. Why is God jealous when we don't make Him the central focus of our lives?

2. Are there things in your life that are more important to you than your relationship with God? What are they? Consider how you spend your time and money.

3. How will you respond to God's jealously?

Scriptures to Read

1. Exodus 20

2. Exodus 32

3. Romans 12

A Moment of Prayer

- Pray that God will help you be more aware that He is jealous for your love.

- Pray that God will help you keep Him as the central focus of your life.

- Pray that God will empower you to live in response to His love.

4

A Perfect Judge

Acts 17:30-31

The times of ignorance God overlooked, but now he commands all people everywhere to repent, because he has fixed a day on which he will judge the world in righteousness by a man whom he has appointed; and of this he has given assurance to all by raising him from the dead.

One day, in the third grade, I was dozing off during one of those really boring school assemblies, when my teacher quietly pulled me out of the auditorium. I was rushed to the principal's office and told to sit down. When I looked up there was a police officer sitting right in front me! For ninety minutes I fearfully answered questions as I was interrogated by this "tough guy" police officer.

Have you ever seen the "good cop, bad cop" interrogation routine on T.V. shows? Well, to this third grader, this interrogation felt like "bad cop," and there was no "good cop." The officer was poking and prodding to see if I had anything to do with graffiti "tags" that had shown up around town and on our school campus. Apparently there was another Gabriel Garcia and their poor detective skills led them to me, a third grader who rarely got into trouble. Even though I was confident in my innocence, I still had images running through my head of standing before a judge and then having a giant jail cell door close behind me with unstoppable force.

Just as I was innocent on that day, I hope you would not have to worry about being punished for breaking the laws of the land if you were forced to stand before a judge. But if you were standing before our holy, righteous, and all-knowing God, would you feel as confident? The truth is that you and I will one day stand before God, our perfect judge.

Sadly, you and I stand guilty and condemned for constantly breaking God's law. James writes, *"For whoever keeps the whole law but fails in one point has become accountable for all of it"* (James 2:10). No matter how hard we try, I feel very confident in saying that none of us has kept the whole law. It is not possible for us. Only Christ has kept the whole law and lived a perfectly sinless life.

Here in the United States, judges would never overlook crimes such as robbery, murder, or rape. If they overlooked these crimes, we would be outraged by their refusal to hand out justice. We would hit the streets in protest if criminals could get away with any crime they desired.

Just as a good and faithful judge is going to hold people accountable, our God will not overlook the sins that we commit against Him and His people. God is a perfectly just God. To overlook these sins, to sweep them under the rug, would be completely against God's nature. God cannot excuse sin and still be God. Because God is just, He must bring justice to our offenses. No matter how big or how small, God cannot allow sin to go unpunished.

The even better news is that while God is just, He is also an extremely loving God. Through the work of Christ on the cross, God is perfectly just and at the same time perfectly gracious. The cross satisfies God's justice and provides us a way to be reconciled to Him. On the cross, sin was not swept under the carpet; it was punished. However, because Jesus took the punishment as our substitute, our sins are forgiven and we can be reconciled to God. But we must accept this gift by believing and following Jesus.

J.I. Packer writes of God and our future judgment:

"We live under his eye, he knows our secrets, and on judgment day the whole of our past life will be played back, as it were, before him, and brought under review. If we know ourselves at all, we know we are not fit to face him. What then are we to do? The New Testament answer is: Call on the coming Judge to be your present Savior."

The call throughout the Bible is to repent and believe. Acts 3:19–20a says, *"Repent, therefore, and turn again, that your sins may be blotted out, that times of refreshing may come from the presence of the Lord."* When we repent and believe in Christ, we will still stand before God and be judged, but we will not be eternally condemned. Christ's perfection will be seen as ours, and His work on the cross will satisfy the justice that God must bring to our sins. Paul powerfully writes, *"Therefore, there is now no condemnation for those who are in Christ Jesus"* (Romans 8:1). In Christ, we avoid the righteous judgment that we fully deserve because He accepted a judgment that He didn't deserve.

The God of the gospel is a God who hates sin so much that He must judge and punish all sin and sinners. Thankfully, He also loves us so much that He was willing to lay our judgment upon Christ, His Son, so that we can be eternally free and eternally reconciled to God.

Our evil works will be brought to justice. We will either choose to pay for our sins, or accept Jesus Christ's payment for our sins. Either way, God's justice will not be thwarted.

Make It Personal

1. Why does God have to punish sin?

2. What would it say about God if He allowed sin to go unpunished?

3. Since Christ paid for our sin, does that mean that we can keep on sinning? Why or why not?

Scriptures to Read

1. Romans 8

2. Romans 6

3. Acts 17

A Moment of Prayer

- Praise God for being willing to go to the cross and face our deserved judgment.

- Pray for the people in your life who are still condemned in their sin instead of living in the freedom of Christ.

- Pray that God will give you the wisdom needed to share with them the amazing truths of the gospel.

A Gracious God

Exodus 34:5-7

The LORD descended in the cloud and stood with him there, and proclaimed the name of the LORD. The LORD passed before him and proclaimed, "The LORD, the LORD, a God merciful and gracious, slow to anger, and abounding in steadfast love and faithfulness, keeping steadfast love for thousands, forgiving iniquity and transgression and sin, but who will by no means clear the guilty, visiting the iniquity of the fathers on the children and the children's children, to the third and the fourth generation."

At the heart of the gospel, and at the heart of God, is grace. Grace is receiving from God what we very clearly don't deserve—salvation. God is a God of amazing grace. Without grace we have no hope. Without grace there is no forgiveness of sins or reconciliation with God.

In Exodus 34 we see God speaking to Moses as He gives him the Ten Commandments. What we receive from God in these verses is one of the most beautiful descriptions of His character to be found in the Bible. Within these verses we see God's hatred for sin accompanied by His love, forgiveness and grace towards sinners. God always hates sin but He loves the sinner and is always willing to forgive through His salvation plan—the gospel.

If God wasn't a God of grace we would only receive what we deserve. We would not be able to experience any of God's blessings, including having an earthly and eternal relationship with Him. Though God will not allow our sin to go unpunished, in His grace He provides a way for us to live a life of freedom and blessing rather than a life of condemnation.

The amazing message of the gospel is that we receive immeasurable blessings while Jesus Christ received condemnation. Paul writes in the book of Ephesians, *"But God, being rich in mercy, because of the great love with which he loved us, even when were dead in our trespasses, made us alive together with Christ—by grace you have been saved"* (Ephesians 2:4–5). Scripture is clear: God doesn't arbitrarily overlook our sin, but by grace He has offered forgiveness to all who choose to accept it. To experience forgiveness, a new life, and God's grace, we must repent of our sin and place our faith in Jesus Christ.

We are fortunate that God doesn't treat us the way we treat other people. Rather than offering grace, we allow our bitter hearts to dictate our ungodly responses. God is willing to give grace to all. He doesn't care who they are or what they have done. If they are willing to turn from their sin and place their faith in Christ, God pours grace upon them.

Oftentimes, we approach all the blessings that come with knowing God as if they are something we deserve. We may not communicate it out loud, but in the depths of our hearts we believe that God owes us a certain kind of life. Due to an outrageously high view of ourselves, we see ourselves as people who don't need God's grace but instead are worthy of His blessings.

We must humble ourselves and come to understand that what we deserve is God's punishment, and what we undeservingly receive is God's forgiveness through Christ our Savior.

As you reflect on the God of the gospel, be amazed that, despite your sin, God is still willing to give you eternal life through Him. Then respond to this amazing grace by giving grace to others. They may not deserve it, but neither did you.

Make It Personal

1. Without God's grace, what would your life look like? In what ways do you experience grace every day?

2. What does God's grace teach you about the character of God?

3. What can you do to reflect God's character by being a grace-giver to the people in your life?

Scriptures to Read

1. Exodus 34

2. Matthew 18

3. Ephesians 2

A Moment of Prayer

- Pray that God will help you to realize who you are in light of His grace.

- Pray that God's grace will daily bring you to Jesus and His work on the cross.

- Pray that God would help you be a person who gives grace to others.

6

This Is Love

1 John 4:8-11

Anyone who does not love does not know God, because God is love. In this the love of God was made manifest among us, that God sent his only Son into the world, so that we might live through him. In this is love, not that we have loved God but that he loved us and sent his Son to be the propitiation for our sins. Beloved, if God so loved us, we also ought to love one another.

So far, we have seen that God is relational, holy, and just. Now, here in 1 John, we see that God is love. Though we may have some picture of what love is, only God can truly define love. Love isn't the infatuation that you had towards your high school sweetheart, nor is it what gets portrayed in Hollywood's romantic comedies.

As selfish people, we want to define how God should express His love for us. For example, we tend to say and think things like: *"If God really loved me . . .*

"He would provide me with this job."

"I wouldn't be going through a divorce."

"He wouldn't let me go through these financial struggles."

We don't get to define love for God. God defines love for us because God is love. John writes, *"In this is love, not that we have loved God but that he loved us and sent his Son to be the propitiation for our sins."* God has shown His love most clearly through Christ on the cross. Isn't that good enough? Do we need more than forgiveness of sins, a renewed relationship with God, and eternal life? Through Christ, God has proven His love for each and every one of us. He shouldn't have to meet our demands in order for us to continue to believe that He loves us.

In the book of 1 John, the apostle John points out that we aren't reconciled to God because we love God. We were born separated from God and at some point in our lives we all lived contrary to His ways, showing our contempt for our loving Father. Some of us are fortunate enough to have grown up in Christian homes where God was introduced to us from our earliest years. Others of us, however, grew up and did our own thing for much of our life. The point is, we have all been separated from God because of our rebellion towards God; some of you still might be.

How would you respond if someone ignored or even hated you? When someone hurts us, we want nothing to do with them. Compare that to our relationship with God. We have hurt, offended, and even shown complete disregard for God. Yet, despite all of that, God displays His love for us. Our rejection, and even hatred, is God's canvas to communicate true love. In the midst of our complete disregard for God, His love shines through brightly as He sends His Son so that we can be brought into a real, authentic, and loving relationship with God.

Hearing that God loves you may seem clichéd; something you have heard over and over since you were a kid. However, without God's love we would be completely lost. We would have no hope in this world and no hope for all of eternity. Without God's love we would face His justice, be declared guilty of breaking God's standards, and be sentenced to eternal death. It is only through God's love that we have the opportunity to be forgiven and declared righteous through Christ.

You may not believe it, but your love has limits. There is a certain point where your love will run dry. That's true even for those we think we could never stop loving, such as our own children. However, God's love never runs dry. It is always flowing. No matter who you are or what you've done, there is nothing that can keep God from showering you with His love—except when you choose to reject God. Don't allow your past mistakes to keep you from experiencing the grace and love of God. Christ went to the cross to forgive those mistakes.

God has shown His love to you. If you have not chosen to put your faith in Jesus, I urge you to accept Him and rejoice in His love.

God is love. His love for us is displayed in no greater way than by going to the cross so that those who repent and believe will be brought into a glorious relationship with the Creator of the universe. How do we respond to this love? Jesus says that we are to *"love the Lord your God with all your heart and with all your soul and with all your mind. This is the great and first commandment. And a second is like it: You shall love your neighbor as yourself"* (Matthew 22:37–39). You've been shown astounding love. In response, be led by God's Spirit to love God and to love others.

Make It Personal

1. In what ways do you take God's love for granted?

2. The cross is certainly God's greatest act of love, but what are other ways that God has shown His love towards us?

3. What are two specific ways you can respond to God's love by loving Him, and what are two specific ways you can love others?

Scriptures to Read

1. 1 John 3

2. Matthew 22

3. 1 John 4

A Moment of Prayer

- Pray that God will help you to fully comprehend His love for you.

- Pray that you would see that at the center of God's love is the cross.

- Pray that God will show you simple and practical ways you can love Him and love others and that you will have the desire and courage to act on them.

Section Two

The Grand Dilemma

Although God loves us and deeply wants a relationship with us, He cannot overlook our sin. We have all sinned and God must punish sin. This is the Grand Dilemma.

Romans 3:10–20

As it is written:
"None is righteous, no, not one;
no one understands; no one seeks for God.
All have turned aside; together they have become worthless;
no one does good, not even one."
"Their throat is an open grave;
they use their tongues to deceive."
"The venom of asps is under their lips."
"Their mouth is full of curses and bitterness."
"Their feet are swift to shed blood;
in their paths are ruin and misery,
and the way of peace they have not known."
"There is no fear of God before their eyes."

Now we know that whatever the law says it speaks to those who are under the law, so that every mouth may be stopped, and the whole world may be held accountable to God. For by works of the law no human being will be justified in his sight, since through the law comes knowledge of sin.

7

Sin Enters the World

Genesis 3:2-6

*And the woman said to the serpent, "We may eat of the fruit
of the trees in the garden, but God said, 'You shall not
eat of the fruit of the tree that is in the midst of the garden,
neither shall you touch it, lest you die.'"
But the serpent said to the woman, "You will not surely die.
For God knows that when you eat of it your eyes will be opened,
and you will be like God, knowing good and evil."
So when the woman saw that the tree was good for food,
and that it was a delight to the eyes, and that the tree was to be
desired to make one wise, she took of its fruit and ate, and she
also gave some to her husband who was with her, and he ate.*

We live in the midst of broken relationships. We can all think
of people that we loved and cared for, who meant the world to
us, but over the course of time our relationships with them were
strained or broken. There is something deep inside of us that
knows this is wrong; that we are not created to have broken relationships. In fact, we often do whatever it takes to try and restore
these relationships.

As we look at Genesis 3, we see that relationships have been
strained and broken from the beginning of time. The first broken
relationship was the one that was meant to exist between God
and man. In the first two chapters of the Bible, everything was
great, but by the third chapter, Adam and Eve show their mis-
trust of God by deliberately ignoring His commands. Through
this one act, sin entered the world. From this point on, sin, in
all its evilness, becomes part of the fabric of our everyday life.

45

Genesis 6:5 says, *"The LORD saw that the wickedness of man was great in the earth, and that every intention of the thoughts of his heart was only evil continually."*

It is often easy for us to nonchalantly talk about sin without truly thinking through its implications. We will not appreciate how revolutionary the gospel is until we build a strong understanding of what sin is and, more specifically, what it does to our relationship with God.

Our sin doesn't come without consequences. It is because of our sin that you and I need the Savior Jesus Christ. Let's examine a few of the major consequences of Adam and Eve's decision to sin and disobey God:

1. There was immediate shame (Genesis 3:7).
2. There was distance from God (Genesis 3:8).
3. For the woman, there was the consequence of pain in child-bearing (Genesis 3:16).
4. For the man, work would be a struggle for survival and a great hardship (Genesis 3:17).
5. For all of humanity, there was the consequence of physical death and possible eternal death (Genesis 3:19).

Though the sins of Adam and Eve may seem completely distant to us, we know that we are just as guilty. Paul famously tells the Romans, *"for all have sinned and fall short of the glory of God"* (Romans 3:23). There isn't a single person who has walked this Earth, besides Jesus Christ himself, who has not fallen short of God's standards of holiness and righteousness. Just as Adam and Eve lived disobediently, so you and I constantly find ourselves choosing to live according to our own desires rather than living according to the desires of the Lord.

Theologian John Stott said about sin, "The emphasis of Scripture, however, is on the godless self-centeredness of sin. Every sin is a breach of what Jesus called 'the first and great commandment,' not just by failing to love God with all our being but by actively refusing to acknowledge and obey him as our Creator and Lord."

When you sin, you are rejecting God as your Creator and Lord. Have you humbled yourself before God, admitted your disobedient ways, and acknowledged Him as Creator and Lord?

In Colossians 1:21–22, Paul writes, *"And you, who once were alienated and hostile in mind, doing evil deeds, he has now reconciled in his body of flesh by his death, in order to present you holy and blameless and above reproach before him."* God has recognized our evil deeds, and due to His supreme holiness, He cannot allow these wicked works to go unpunished. However, the gospel's good news is that God sent Christ to be punished in our place so that we could be restored back to a perfect relationship with Him. Jesus did this by conquering sin and its punishment of death through His own death on the cross and resurrection.

Sin is at the heart of our broken relationships. It is because we sin against each other that there is division and disunity. Sin is also at the heart of our broken relationship with God. However, we can rejoice because Christ has freed us from the bondage of sin and reconciled us into a perfect relationship with God.

Make It Personal

1. What can you do to be more aware of your acts of sin and their consequences?

2. When was the last time you confessed and repented of your specific sins before God?

3. What can you do to be reconciled with someone you have a strained or broken relationship with? How does that reflect what Christ has done for you?

Scriptures to Read

1. Genesis 3

2. Romans 3

3. Genesis 6

A Moment of Prayer

- Pray that God will help you to deepen your understanding of sin.

- Pray that you would become more aware of the consequences of your sin.

- Pray that God will help you picture Christ on the cross whenever you are tempted to sin.

8

Lover of Sin

Colossians 3:5-10

*Put to death therefore what is earthly in you: sexual immorality,
impurity, passion, evil desire, and covetousness, which is idolatry.
On account of these the wrath of God is coming. In these you too
once walked, when you were living in them. But now you must
put them all away: anger, wrath, malice, slander, and obscene talk
from your mouth. Do not lie to one another, seeing that you have
put off the old self with its practices and have put on the new self,
which is being renewed in knowledge after the image of its creator.*

I don't love broccoli, but I will eat it every once in a while. I do
love cheesecake. I know it is not healthy on any level. I know it's
1,000 calories per slice. But I will eat it anyway and enjoy every
bite of it. Sin isn't like broccoli. Sin is like cheesecake, and before
Christ, we loved sin.

As we build a strong understanding of sin, let's be clear, sin
is something that we are really good at. Sin is not something
we have dabbled in or something we did every once in awhile.
Though we were blind to our sinful passions, God's Word teaches
that, before Christ, we loved to sin and we loved our lifestyle of
sin.

Satan would love to convince us that we really are good people.
He would love to make us believe that we're not that bad. If we
lie, it's *only* little white lies, and if we raise our voices in anger,
it's *only* once in awhile. But that's not what the Bible teaches us,
and that's not what our lives reflect upon closer examination. We
have all wandered off and lived outside of God's will in complete
rebellion. Have you seen yourself as a lover of sin?

As Colossians 3:5–10 states, before we put our faith in Jesus we loved to go against God's ways, and it was leading us towards God's wrath. We deserve God's wrath, not just because we messed up every once in a while, but because we chose sin over obedience and because we chose self over God. Our entire worldview and framework for life was completely contrary to the life God created us to live. We deserve eternal punishment from our holy God due to our unholy sin. However, when we respond to the good news of the gospel with repentance and faith, by God's grace, His wrath is diverted from us and directed towards Christ on the cross.

Colossians 3 calls us to put off the *"old self."* We have to completely throw off all of our sin-loving habits: our love of gossip, our love of laziness, our love of cheating, our love of living according to our will rather than the will of God. The scripture continues, stating that we should instead *"put on the new self."* The new self is our life in Christ and it is a new desire to *turn from* that which is sinful and *run towards* that which is holy. Though we used to love sin, we must now hate it.

Considering how much we loved our old lives outside of Christ and how much we loved sin, putting it off is not easy. If we think that putting our old life to death will be easy, Satan has us right where he wants us, and sooner or later we will fall back into his temptations. We must recognize how lost we were, and how much sin was ingrained in our lives, so that we will turn to God and become completely dependent upon Him to strengthen us in our moments of weakness.

On the cross, Christ conquered the power of sin. Though we are still tempted on a daily basis, we now have the supernatural power of the Holy Spirit giving us the ability to leave the sinful lifestyle we once cherished.

One of the signs that the gospel has truly impacted our lives is that we begin to accurately see what we were before Christ. We weren't people who were just a little lost. We were completely lost. We weren't people who accidentally sinned. We were people who loved sin. The more we understand our love for sin, the more we will recognize our need for a Savior and find in Him all the strength we need to turn from a lifestyle that will only lead us towards God's wrath.

Make It Personal

1. Why is it important to fully understand our love for sin?

2. What happens if we take our sin too lightly?

3. To turn more closely towards God, what do you need to "put off"? What do you need to "put on"?

Scriptures to Read

1. Luke 15

2. Colossians 3

3. Psalm 119

A Moment of Prayer

- Pray that God will continue to empower you through Christ to leave your old life and put on your new life.

- Pray that God would help you to hate the sin in your life.

- Praise God that He loves you despite your true character.

9

Dead in Sin

Ephesians 2:1-3

And you were dead in the trespasses and sins in which you once walked, following the course of this world, following the prince of the power of the air, the spirit that is now at work in the sons of disobedience—among whom we all once lived in the passions of our flesh, carrying out the desires of the body and the mind, and were by nature children of wrath, like the rest of mankind.

Sometimes we all need a dose of reality. I need someone to remind me that I can't sing. It is one thing to sing during a worship service, but it's another thing when I bring my talents to the office or local grocery store. I know that I truly am not gifted in this area, but sometimes I forget. That is why, every now and then, I need a good brother or sister to remind me of my lack of talent.

As we reflect on our scripture passage from Ephesians 2, we see Paul giving us a reality check. He reminds us of our complete wickedness outside of Jesus Christ due to the sin that plagues us. Paul is very straightforward in writing that we all are, or once were, *"dead in (our) trespasses and sins."* Sin is a cancer that plagues and kills us, but Christ's life, death and resurrection can save us. Christ is our cure.

Being "dead" in our sins doesn't mean that we are physically dead. It points to what will happen beyond our physical death. Being dead in sin refers to our complete inability to glorify God, and it points to an eternal death—a death that we are already beginning to experience as a reality in our lives today. A life that has no hope of honoring God and no hope of being reconciled to God is a dead life. You may be the healthiest guy or gal on the block. You may be able to run marathons while lifting dumbbells at the same time. But if you are living outside of Christ, you are spiritually dead.

In Ephesians 2, Paul gives us a glimpse of what it looks like to live a dead life:

1. We're consumed with following the ways of the world.
2. Instead of following the lordship of God, we are following the leadership of Satan.
3. Instead of being led by the Spirit, we act upon the impulses of our sinful flesh, mind, and heart.

In another one of his letters, Paul explains how we arrived at our current situation, and how we can get out of it.

"But in fact Christ has been raised from the dead, the firstfruits of those who have fallen asleep. For as by a man came death, by a man has come also the resurrection of the dead. For as in Adam all die, so also in Christ shall all be made alive. But each in his own order: Christ the firstfruits, then at his coming those who belong to Christ." (1 Corinthians 15:20–23)

Paul explains that we are all in the historical family line of Adam, which explains our sin and its result in death. However, through repentance and faith in Christ, we are placed in the line of Christ, made alive, and given a new, resurrected life. We all start in Adam's line, but we have the choice of joining the line of Christ.

Allowing ourselves to remain spiritually dead means that, at the core, we don't care about God or His will. Think about how you feel when someone disregards your feelings or desires. That is what we are doing to God when we disregard His desire to be the focal point of our all-consuming worship or when we disregard His desire for us to be others-focused rather than self-focused. Though we may evaluate ourselves as "pretty good people," the scriptures lay out a bleaker account. The scriptures declare us to be a wicked people who ignore the will of God and live for ourselves and the will of Satan.

Let me ask you, if you never forgot what God saved you from, would it make a difference on how you view and live life now? Though we may be years removed from the days when we lived in the kind of "wickedness" Paul refers to, it is vitally important to our Christian walk that we remember what we've been saved from, and how we were saved—not by works, but by grace, through Christ's wrath-bearing work on the cross. For the Christian, it is important to be reminded daily of these truths, allowing them to bring us back to our knees in worship of our God who saw fit to save us, even when we were "dead."

If you are not a follower of Christ, I hope you have seen from these scriptures that all people, including yourself, are *"dead,"* but through Christ we are made alive again. I pray that God keeps opening your heart and mind to the biblical truth that you are doomed without God and that there is nothing you can do to get right with God except to put your faith in the perfect life, substitutionary death, and resurrection of Jesus Christ. It is through Christ's death that we can have hope for a meaningful life here on earth and an eternal life with God.

It is faith and only faith in the revolutionary message of the gospel that transfers us from death to an abundant life in Christ. The gospel truly is the most forceful reality that we will ever encounter. It has the power to resurrect us to a full life here on earth and, one day, to an eternal life with God.

Make It Personal

1. Are you dead in your sins or are you alive in Christ? What does that mean to you?

2. According to the Bible, what does it mean to be "dead"?

3. How can your awareness of what you were saved from, and how you were saved, inspire your worship of God?

4. Do you need to move from "death" to life? Turn to "Making the Greatest Decision Ever" on page 199 for guidance on putting your life in Jesus' hands.

Scriptures to Read

1. Ephesians 2

2. Romans 5

3. 1 Corinthians 15

A Moment of Prayer

- Pray that God would soften your heart towards those without Christ.

- Pray that God would continue to awaken your heart so that it becomes more passionate about the gospel.

- Praise God for the work He has done to save you from death and bring you back to life.

10

God's Hatred of Sin

Psalm 51:1-4

Have mercy on me, O God, according to your steadfast love;
according to your abundant mercy blot out my transgressions.
Wash me thoroughly from my iniquity, and cleanse me
from my sin! For I know my transgressions, and my sin
is ever before me. Against you, you only, have I sinned
and done what is evil in your sight, so that you may be
justified in your words and blameless in your judgment.

Reading Psalm 51 gives us a transparent picture into the heart and soul of King David. When it comes to David's recognition of how his transgressions have deeply offended God, we see a great deal of self-awareness in this Psalm. Though David was a great king, and an historic figure of the Bible, he had flaws like everyone else. But when he truly came into contact with our wonderfully holy God, he was humbled by his unholiness. The same will be true for us.

It is our pride, it seems, that keeps us from being truly self-aware about who we really are and about the things we have done to turn our backs on God. But until we understand our wretchedness, we will never comprehend our need for the spotless Lamb who can take away our sins.

As we examine our lives, in contrast to the Word of God, we should be broken by the commitment we have towards sinning against God. Once we truly see the sin that is plaguing our lives, we should allow God to humble us and then be moved to cry out like David, *"Wash me thoroughly from my iniquity, and cleanse me from my sin!"*

In Psalm 51, we not only see David's self-awareness of sin, which is a monumental first step, we also can see that he has a healthy understanding of how God views his sin. David says, *"against you, you only, have I sinned and done what is evil in your sight."* David recognizes that sin isn't just a minor irritation to God like a small pebble in your shoe would be, nor is it just an annoyance to God like traffic jams or long lines in the grocery store are to us. Absolutely not! David recognizes that sin is an absolute evil in the sight of God.

Most of us can comprehend the idea of sin being evil. However, when we think of sin, what comes to the forefront of our minds are things like rape, murder, genocide, war, child abuse, and other horrific things that people are capable of doing. Yes, God hates these sins and they are evil in His eyes, but so are the sins that you and I live with day in and day out, sins like gossip, anger, lies, laziness, worry, and pride.

Very rarely do we think of our sins as something that God hates. Rather, it is everyone else's sins that are detestable to God. We must face the fact that no matter how "big" or "small" our sins are they are all hated by God. To make ourselves feel better, we like to believe that there are different levels of sin—those that are sort of bad, those that are pretty bad, and those that are horrific—and it's only the really bad ones that we have to worry about. However, in God's eyes every sin is disobedient and disrespectful towards Him.

God hates sin. Do you? As you move towards spiritual maturity, you must allow the Holy Spirit to help you view your sin the way God views your sin. What sin are you currently overlooking? Your sin might not seem evil and wicked, but as you grow in your love for the gospel, God will stir inside of you a passion to hate *all* sin.

Our spiritual maturity will continue to increase as we allow God to move us from being nonchalant about our sin to being people that have a great determination to hate, fight, and run from sin. The more we learn to hate sin, the more we will depend on the Holy Spirit to empower us to live a life committed to honoring and glorifying God.

Whether we are walking with Christ or not, let us learn from David as we seek to become keenly aware, and to even hate, our sin. As David cried out for mercy, we too can cry out for mercy from the One who took on our sin so that we would be cleansed from the dirty filth of our transgressions. We can cry out to Jesus, who upon the cross became sin for us so that we could find a way back to our holy God.

Make It Personal

1. Why do you believe God hates our sin?

2. How can you become more aware of your sin?

3. Does it hurt you that you have hurt God through your sin?

Scriptures to Read

1. Ephesians 2

2. Romans 5

3. 1 Corinthians 15

A Moment of Prayer

- Pray that God would help you to fully see how He views all sin.

- Pray that God would build a spirit of humility in you so that you can continually be more aware of your disobedience to God and be willing to confess and turn from it.

- Praise God for providing Jesus Christ as the ultimate sacrifice that cleanses us from our sins.

11

God's Wrath

Romans 2:5-8

*But because of your hard and impenitent heart you are storing
up wrath for yourself on the day of wrath when God's righteous
judgment will be revealed. He will render to each one according
to his works: to those who by patience in well-doing seek for
glory and honor and immortality, he will give eternal life;
but for those who are self-seeking and do not obey the truth,
but obey unrighteousness, there will be wrath and fury.*

Sometimes, in order to make ourselves feel better about the
fact that we have turned our backs on God, we view God as if
He were a warm, fuzzy teddy bear. This is unbiblical. The reason
we build our own views of God is that we want God to always
accept and love us no matter what we do. Yes, a part of God's
character is His love and grace, but God cannot allow sin to go
unpunished. As we have seen, and as we will continue to see,
a part of God's character is His holy and righteous justice. God's
justice means that no matter how big or small our sin is, God
must punish it.

Just as much as God is love, God is also just. Romans 2:5-8
speaks of God's justice in terms of His wrath and points to
a future day when unbelievers will experience that wrath for all
of eternity. Although it is true that God is love, that He is our
friend, and that He is gracious and forgiving, the gospel will not
be fully transforming if we shy away from the biblical truth of
God's wrath.

It is through the wrath of God that His need for justice is
satisfied. Our most clear depiction of God's wrath is seen in what
Jesus Christ went through on the cross. Though the physical

aspect of the cross was totally gruesome, Jesus' experience of God's wrath goes beyond our full comprehension. Jesus' suffering went far beyond the incredible pain of nails, thorns, beating, and the overall experience of being hung on a cross; it also included His experience of having our sins placed upon Him. We cannot even begin to imagine the excruciating pain of the cross, but that wasn't the worst of it. The worst was that for the first time Jesus was experiencing total separation from God as God's wrath was poured out on Him because of our sins.

Although other men have been crucified, Jesus experienced something no one else ever has as He died on that cross; something that changed the course of all human history. Jerry Bridges writes, "We do not know all that transpired during those three terrible hours when Jesus endured the wrath of God. Scripture draws a veil over them for the most part. We do know that the physical suffering Jesus endured was only a feeble picture of the suffering of His soul."

On the cross, the wrath of God was poured out on Christ. The truth that we must all uncomfortably reflect on is that this dark cloud of God's wrath hovers over each and every one of us until we place our faith in Christ. Paul writes in Romans 1:18, *"For the wrath of God is revealed from heaven against all ungodliness and unrighteousness of men, who by their unrighteousness suppress the truth."* If we choose to turn our backs on Christ and the good news of the gospel, we will experience this dark and thunderous cloud of God's wrath being poured out on us for all of eternity. However, if we choose to place our faith completely in Christ, the dark cloud is removed because Christ absorbed the fullness of God's wrath on our behalf. The amazing accomplishment of the cross is that God's wrath can be removed from us if we choose to place our trust fully in the one who stood condemned in our place.

We can constantly see in scripture God's hatred for sin but His love for people. Psalm 145:20 is one example where we see both God's love and wrath. *"The Lord preserves all who love him but all the wicked he will destroy."* When we put our faith in Jesus and His work on the cross, we allow Him to remove God's wrath from our life. When we choose to do that, our sins will be forgiven, and we will be declared innocent and righteous by God. The prophet Isaiah writes, *"But he was wounded for our transgressions; he was crushed for our iniquities; upon him was the chastisement that brought us peace, and with his stripes we are healed"* (Isaiah 53:5). It is because of the wrath-bearing work of Christ that we can have the privilege of entering into a relationship with God.

We should run from God's wrath by running to Jesus, but by no means should we run from and deny the truth of God's punishment of sin. Christ stood in our place and received the condemnation He didn't deserve so that we would receive the freedom we don't deserve. As we continue to comprehend the justice we have been saved from, the gospel will surely take root and continue an all-transforming work on our lives for His glory.

Make It Personal

1. Why do you think we often don't talk about, study, or reflect on God's wrath?

2. How can reflecting on God's wrath help us to understand and rejoice in the gospel?

3. What can you do today to thank God for providing a substitute to take your place in receiving God's wrath?

Scriptures to Read

1. Isaiah 53

2. Romans 1

3. Romans 2

A Moment of Prayer

- Pray that God will help you see the spiritual reality of the cross: that upon Christ God's wrath was poured out for our sins.

- Pray that God would break your heart for the people that are still living under His wrath.

- Pray that you will never take for granted what Christ did for you on the cross.

Section Three

Rescued by Christ

Though we have all wandered away, the good news is that we have a God who loves us so much that He sent His Son to the cross so that we could be rescued from the condemnation of our sin.

Isaiah 53:4–6

Surely he has borne our griefs
and carried our sorrows;
yet we esteemed him stricken,
smitten by God, and afflicted.
But he was wounded for our transgressions;
he was crushed for our iniquities;
upon him was the chastisement that brought us peace,
and with his stripes we are healed.
All we like sheep have gone astray;
we have turned—every one—to his own way;
and the LORD has laid on him
the iniquity of us all.

12

God Takes Initiative

Galatians 4:4-5

But when the fullness of time had come, God sent forth his Son, born of woman, born under the law, to redeem those who were under the law, so that we might receive adoption as sons.

I don't know much about relationships, but I do know that a woman always feels cherished when a man takes the initiative to show his interest in her. He may ask her out for coffee, show up at her office with flowers, or just say, "Girl, I like you." Well, I'm not sure if that last one actually works, but I know that all people appreciate it when someone takes the initiative to show them that they are cared for and loved.

The gospel shows us how God has taken the initiative. From eternity past, God designed a way to solve the biggest problem that exists in this world, sin. All of the scriptures speak to the defining moment when this problem was reversed as man's sins were transferred and placed on Jesus while on the cross.

The root of all the world's problems is sin. Sin is the disease that has infected the world and each and every one of us. Even with all the brilliant people that we have in this world, people who solve foreign crises, who cure diseases, who explore the galaxies, no one has, or will ever be able to, solve the problem of sin. However, in God's love and mercy, He took the initiative to cure our debilitating problem of sin and give us hope for our eternal future.

Galatians 4:4-5 reminds us that it was God's perfect orchestration to send His Son into human history to be our Redeemer and set us free from the captivity of sin. It was never our idea.

As early as the third chapter of Genesis we see that God had a plan to set sinners free. In that chapter, the Lord looks forward to a day when the serpent, Satan, will be crushed by a seed that would come through the woman. This seed would be Jesus. In Genesis 3:15 God says to the serpent, *"I will put enmity between you and the woman, and between your offspring and her offspring; he shall bruise your head, and you shall bruise his heel."* Some refer to this passage as the first gospel message.

Because of His love for the world, God took the initiative and sent forth His Son into a broken and fallen creation to be mocked and humiliated and to receive God the Father's righteous wrath. Upon repentance and faith in Christ as our Messiah, not only are our sins forgiven, but we are adopted into the family of God. Paul writes, *"And because you are sons, God has sent the Spirit of his Son into our hearts, crying, 'Abba! Father!' So you are no longer a slave, but a son, and if a son, then an heir through God"* (Galatians 4:6–7). One of the greatest blessings of the gospel is that, through Christ, we are adopted and welcomed into God's family. God becomes our Father and we become His children. Without God's perfect plan, and without God being willing to send forth His Son, we would be people without hope under the wrath of God.

Paul writes to the Ephesians,

> *"And you were dead in the trespasses and sins in which you once walked, following the course of this world, following the prince of the power of the air, the spirit that is now at work in the sons of disobedience—among whom we all once lived in the passions of our flesh, carrying out the desires of the body and the mind, and were by nature children of wrath, like the rest of mankind."* (Ephesians 2:1–3)

We are children of God's wrath until we accept Christ; with Christ, we become children of God.

I pray that God will give us the vision to see how much we are loved by Him as He takes the initiative to redeem us from the brokenness of our sin. And I pray that we would understand that it is God who does all the work. We have done nothing to earn God's amazing blessings, yet we receive them when we repent and put our trust in God's plan to reconcile us to Himself through Jesus Christ. Though we are all sinners, God was willing to create a way so that we could be adopted into His family.

Make It Personal

1. Where would we be if God had not devised a salvation plan?

2. What does it say about the character of God that He took the initiative to save us?

3. Are you rejoicing and thankful for the plan that God has designed and executed through the life, death, and resurrection of Jesus Christ?

Scriptures to Read

1. Galatians 3

2. Galatians 4

3. Ephesians 2

A Moment of Prayer

- Pray that God will continue to show you that the gospel is all about Him and His work.

- Pray that you would live in the reality of being adopted into God's family.

- Pray that God would never allow you to forget the amazing truths of the gospel.

13

Jesus Comes to Save

Luke 19:10

For the Son of Man came to seek and to save the lost.

As a little kid growing up, I cherished nothing more than the little puppy dog my parents brought home for my brother and me. I remember how, when the dog was just a few weeks old, it would sleep on my stomach as I lay on the ground. However, during one hot summer, it ran away. Every day, frantically and fearfully, my brother and I would go on "missions" through the neighborhood, searching for this very valuable member of our family. As much as we would have loved to have just sat back in our air-conditioned home and waited for her to come back, we knew we needed to make an effort and do something.

As we think about the life of Jesus Christ, we must see that He is on a very specific mission. As Luke 19:10 points out, Jesus is on a mission to *"save the lost."* We need to be saved because we have wandered away from God our Father and are spiritually lost. Just as my dog wandered off, *"we like sheep have gone astray; we have turned—every one—to his own way"* (Isaiah 53:6).

In Luke 15 there is a parable that refers to Jesus' mission of searching for us. Jesus says:

> *"What man of you, having a hundred sheep, if he has lost one of them, does not leave the ninety-nine in the open country, and go after the one that is lost, until he finds it? And when he has found it, he lays it on his shoulders, rejoicing. And when*

he comes home, he calls together his friends and his neighbors, saying to them, 'Rejoice with me, for I have found my sheep that was lost.'" (Luke 15:4–6)

Just as my brother and I went on our "missions" to save our dog, so God sends His Son Jesus Christ to save us. The thing about being spiritually lost is that there is nothing we can do to save ourselves. No matter how hard we try, we cannot find our way back to God on our own. That's why we are in need of a Savior, someone who is willing and able to rescue us from our "lostness." So, Jesus comes on a very specific mission. He wasn't here to check out the scenery. He wasn't here to drink lattes. He left His position in heaven and became a man to "seek and save the lost." Every second of His life, Jesus worked towards accomplishing His mission; a mission He completed through His perfect life, death on the cross, and resurrection from the grave. Jesus came to this world to die on a cross and rise three days later so that humanity could be rescued from its own wickedness.

In another of Jesus' parables, we see the heart of a father who was reconciled to his cherished, but lost, son.

"But the father said to his servants 'Bring quickly the best robe, and put it on him, and put a ring on his hand, and shoes on his feet. And bring the fattened calf and kill it, and let us eat and celebrate. For this my son was dead, and is alive again; he was lost, and is found.' And they began to celebrate." (Luke 15:22–24)

God not only loved us so much that He sent His Son on a mission to save us, He also rejoices when we are found. My brother and I celebrated when we found our dog that summer, but our God truly celebrates when we are reconciled with Him.

My brother and I looked for our dog because she was loved, and a shepherd looks for lost sheep because they are important to him. For these same reasons, God the Father sent His Son on a mission to rescue us and reconcile us to Himself for all eternity.

Let us rejoice in the truth that we have a God who loves and values us so much that He sent His Son to the cross on the greatest rescue mission ever accomplished.

Make It Personal

1. If you had a child who was lost in the wilderness, what lengths would you go to in your efforts to find him or her?

2. Do you live with an awareness of your need to be rescued by God? How does that awareness affect the time and commitment you put into building your relationship with God?

3. Does your heart break for people who are still spiritually lost?

Scriptures to Read

1. Luke 15

2. 1 Peter 2

3. 1 Timothy 2

A Moment of Prayer

- Pray that God would instill in your spirit a great appreciation for what Christ did to come and rescue you.

- Pray that we would be just as passionate about the lost as God is.

- Pray that we would live a lifestyle of rejoicing with our Father as we are reunited with Him.

14

Christ Our Substitute

Isaiah 53:4–6

Surely he has borne our griefs and carried our sorrows; yet we esteemed him stricken, smitten by God, and afflicted. But he was wounded for our transgressions; he was crushed for our iniquities; upon him was the chastisement that brought us peace, and with his stripes we are healed. All we like sheep have gone astray; we have turned—every one—to his own way; and the LORD has laid on him the iniquity of us all.

Back in the day, I used to be a pretty intense basketball player. I was passionate about basketball and worked really hard at it. When I was playing, there was nothing more irritating to me than to be pulled out of the game by my coach. As I saw the substitute getting off the bench and taking off his warm-ups, resentment would start building in my heart. I hated being pulled out of a game and replaced by someone else.

The gospel teaches us that there is no good news without substitution. When Jesus Christ went to the cross in our place, He became our substitute. Isaiah wrote, *"he was wounded for our transgressions; he was crushed for our iniquities."* Instead of us being eternally wounded for our transgressions and crushed for our iniquities, we have a Savior who undeservedly took on God's wrath in our place so that we can have forgiveness of sins and reconciliation with God.

One reason that I hated being pulled out of basketball games was that I believed I had earned the right to keep playing. I had put in the hard work, and I thought my hard work should be rewarded. Luckily for us, God doesn't give us what we deserve.

When we look at what Christ experienced on the cross, we see what we have truly earned. The physical brutality of Jesus' crucifixion and, worse, the spiritual brutality of Jesus having to experience God's wrath give us a clear picture of what we deserve.

Oftentimes, we believe that we are worthy of all the blessings and eternal life God offers. However, the more we mature in the truths of the gospel, the more we realize that every blessing we receive from God is completely undeserved and comes only by His grace. Mark Dever writes, "Jesus did not sin; He died the death we deserve in order to bear our iniquities and our transgressions, to bear God's correct and right penalty against them. When that work was done, God raised him from the dead and highly exalted him to show that he accepted the sacrifice and that all of Jesus' claims were true." It is because of Christ's amazing work on the cross, and the miracle of the resurrection, that you and I can rejoice that we have the opportunity to turn from our sin and place our faith fully in Christ.

Isaiah wrote, *"upon him was the chastisement that brought us peace, and with his stripes we are healed."* The gospel is full of blessings, but those blessings occur only because of the substitution of Christ. Isaiah points out that through the work of Christ, God's children will experience both peace and healing. The peace we experience is peace with God; which is the greatest peace a person can know. Since the blood of Christ covers the sins of those who trust in Him, the transgressions that cause hostility between man and God are removed. There is now peace instead of hostility. The healing we experience is a spiritual healing. Rather than being spiritually dead, we are resurrected to a brand new life here on earth and we look forward to being resurrected to the new heaven and new earth where we will be physically restored for all of eternity.

As we reflect upon Isaiah 53:4–6, let us see that salvation is available only through the substitutionary life and death of Christ. When we put our faith in Jesus and repent of our sinful ways, Christ's death is counted towards our forgiveness and His life is counted towards our righteousness.

Let us grow in gratefulness towards God, who was willing to take us out of the game and substitute Christ in our place so that He would receive what we deserved and we would receive what we don't deserve. That's a substitution I won't argue with.

Make It Personal

1. What does it mean that Christ is our substitute?

2. What imagery stands out to you the most from Isaiah 53:4–6?

3. How is God causing you to fall more in love with Christ and more in love with the gospel?

Scriptures to Read

1. Isaiah 53

2. 1 Corinthians 15

3. John 14

A Moment of Prayer

- Pray that God would help you to more fully comprehend what Christ's substitutionary death means.

- Pray that you see that true peace and healing come only through Christ.

- Pray that God would continue to awaken you to fully experience, and become more passionate about, the good news of the gospel.

15

Justified by Faith

Romans 5:1-2

Therefore, since we have been justified by faith, we have peace with God through our Lord Jesus Christ. Through him we have also obtained access by faith into this grace in which we stand, and we rejoice in hope of the glory of God.

I remember the first time I lied to my parents. I lied so that I could go to my friend's house down the street and play on their makeshift slip-and-slide. That night, after my parents became aware of my scheme, I stood before them in great fear because I knew I was completely guilty. I stood there condemned for my disobedient actions and there was nothing I could do to get out of my judgment. Just as I stood before my parents that evening awaiting their judgment, you and I will stand before our eternal Judge.

In order to be allowed into the presence of God for all eternity, we need to be declared perfectly innocent and perfectly righteous by God. This declaration is what scriptures call "justification." It is only through faith in the gospel's message of Jesus' substitutionary life and death that you and I can be justified. Without the gospel's promise of justification, we are condemned by God.

Justification is a truth found throughout scripture. It helps us understand on a deeper level what Christ has done for us by going to the cross to pay the penalty for our disobedience. Leon Morris writes that the understanding of justification is strongly linked with "the concept of judgment day, a day when all people will be tried before God with the result that some will be adjudged righteous (i.e., be justified) and others condemned." The bottom line is that we will be either condemned for our own efforts, or justified by Christ's efforts.

Very simply, without Christ we will be condemned. If we fail to repent and place our faith in Christ, we will rightfully be declared guilty and given the eternal punishment that we have earned. However, Romans 5:1 says that Christians *"have been justified by faith."* It is our faith that brings us justification; faith in the life, death, and resurrection of Jesus Christ.

Through our faith in Christ, not only are we declared innocent of our offenses against God, but we are also seen as being perfectly righteous. The reason we can be declared innocent is that Christ was condemned and punished in our place. And the reason we can be declared righteous is that Christ lived a perfectly holy life for us.

Is your faith in Christ and Christ alone? This declaration of justification is given to you based only on your faith in Jesus Christ. You cannot be declared innocent and righteous apart from faith in the gospel's good news about Jesus Christ.

Paul writes very famously in Romans 8:1, *"There is therefore now no condemnation for those who are in Christ Jesus."* That is great news! You and I have the opportunity to be declared innocent and righteous rather than condemned, all because of what Christ did for us.

Let us meditate on two truths that lead to our justification.

1. Christ lived a perfectly holy and righteous life. Therefore, through faith in Christ, we are seen as having the righteousness of Jesus.
2. Christ has gone to the cross, taken upon himself our sins, and received the punishment that those sins deserve. Therefore, through faith in Christ, we are seen as perfectly innocent of our past offenses.

When we place our faith in Christ, we are fully justified, and when, one day, we stand before our perfect Judge, we will not have to fearfully stand condemned due to our disobedient behavior. Instead, we will be standing on the perfect behavior of Jesus and declared innocent by God.

Make It Personal

1. What is your response to the good news that God is willing to declare you completely innocent and righteous?

2. What is the gospel's solution to our legal predicament with God as our holy judge?

3. Have you put your faith in the life, death, and resurrection of Jesus Christ? Are you ready to? If so, turn to page 199 for guidance.

Scriptures to Read

1. John 3

2. Romans 3

3. Romans 5

A Moment of Prayer

- Pray that God would open your eyes to see that it is only through the work of Christ that we can be declared innocent and righteous.

- Pray that God would continue to remind you that salvation is through faith alone, not by works.

- Praise God for providing a way to lift the "condemned" charge from us.

16

The Great Trade

2 Corinthians 5:21

For our sake he made him to be sin who knew no sin, so that in him we might become the righteousness of God.

Do you remember lunchtime in elementary school? I can still smell the cafeteria to this day, a little musty and a little like beef stroganoff. My mom packed a lunch for me to bring every day (except on Fridays—Friday was corndog and tater tot day, and like all good Americans, I love hot dogs on a stick).

I remember lunchtime as always being about making a good trade. The lunchroom was like a stock market for ten-year-olds. There was always something in my lunch that was worth trading; perhaps a Twinkie or pudding cup. If I was feeling really bold, I would try to work my magic and trade a piece of fruit. Never being fully satisfied with the lunch my mom packed, I did everything possible to make a trade and, like all good hustlers, I always tried to "trade up."

As we continue to allow the gospel to revolutionize our lives, it is crucial that we become aware of a great trade that has taken place. This trade doesn't involve Twinkies or even stocks and bonds; it has to do with something much more serious, our sin and Christ's righteousness. In God's perfect salvation plan, He provided us with an opportunity to trade up. We give Christ our sin, and Christ gives us His righteousness.

As we have discussed, it is our sin that keeps us separated from God and the abundant life He wants us to live for Him. If God didn't provide a solution, we would all spend an eternity receiving our just punishment. The good news is that God did provide a solution and it involves Christ's righteousness.

When we talk about the righteousness of Christ, we are talking about Christ's perfect life; a life without sin, a life of perfect obedience, a life of complete holiness. Peter wrote it simply: *"He committed no sin, neither was deceit found in his mouth"* (1 Peter 2:22). If we want to have a relationship with God, we have to be completely righteous. Outside of the work of Christ, our chances of living a perfectly righteous life are zero. Since we can't be righteous by our own efforts, we must depend on the work of Jesus Christ.

When we place our faith in Christ and His work, we give Christ our nasty, dirty sin, and He takes on that sin and even pays for that sin by receiving God's wrath on the cross. Theologian Wayne Grudem helps us understand this staggering theological truth by stating, "God imputed our sins to Christ; that is, he thought of them as belonging to Christ, and, since God is the ultimate judge and definer of what really is in the universe, when God thought of our sins as belonging to Christ then in fact they actually did belong to Christ."

In turn, after we give Christ our sin, He gives us His perfect righteousness and his character. In no way do we actually become perfect; however, in God's gracious love, once we put our faith in Christ, God sees us as having the perfection of Christ. It is only through this trade of sin for righteousness that we have the opportunity to be reconciled to God, be adopted into His family, and receive the blessing of eternal life with God.

To my friends who haven't placed their faith in Christ, I hope you see that this ridiculous trade is made only because God loves you and passionately wants to be in a relationship with you. Why else would He allow His Son to leave the joy of a heavenly relationship to endure a fallen world and an excruciating cross? I pray that God will continue to reveal to you the depravity of your sin and the grace He has provided through Christ.

The great trade that we learn about in 2 Corinthians 5:21 is that we give Christ our sin and He gives us His righteousness. This doesn't seem like a fair trade to me, but it's a trade that highlights the grace and love of God. Without receiving the righteousness of Christ we are without hope, without eternal life, and under the condemnation of God. Let us be people who are forever grateful for the righteous life of Jesus Christ and forever grateful that we have a God who is willing to make such a ridiculous trade.

Make It Personal

1. Have you spent time reflecting on the importance of the perfection of Jesus Christ?

2. What does it say about the character of our God that He is willing to trade our sin for His righteousness? Is He worthy of your worship and complete devotion?

3. If Christ hasn't taken your sin upon Himself, are you willing to stand before a just God and take the punishment that you deserve?

Scriptures to Read

1. 1 Peter 2

2. 2 Corinthians 5

A Moment of Prayer

- Pray that you will never take for granted this trade that Christ is willing to make.

- Pray that you will continue to live with a great faith in, and love for, the gospel.

- Praise Christ for taking on our sin.

17

Christ Our Ransom

Mark 10:45

*For even the Son of Man did not come to be served but
to serve, and to give his life as a ransom for many.*

Scriptures offer many different metaphors that help us understand what Christ has done to reconcile us to God and give us new life. In Mark's gospel, Jesus speaks of His work on the cross as a "ransom." When I think of a ransom, I immediately think of those high-paced action movies where the loving father does everything he can to find his kidnapped child. Usually there are a couple of high speed car chases, the father miraculously learns how to use a gun, and the kidnappers want a million-dollar ransom before the young child is released.

How would you feel if you were kidnapped, but no one ever came to rescue you? Scripture reveals that you and I are being held captive by our sin and its judgment. Fortunately, God our Father did what we could not do for ourselves by offering us freedom for our captivity.

Whether we want to admit it or not, before we put our faith in Christ we lived a life enslaved to sin, and because of our sin we awaited a future condemnation. In order to release us from the grips of sin and from our ultimate eternal punishment, a ransom was needed, and Jesus was that ransom.

Mark Dever writes, "Jesus understood his own death as a substitutionary ransom for his people, purchasing their freedom from the bondage of sin. So, Jesus becomes our ransom. He wins our release from sin and judgment by giving his life, by dying. His death would pay the price so that his people might be released." Due to the work of Christ, we have the opportunity to be freed from our condemnation and instead be reconciled to God. Once we turn from our sin in repentance and place our faith in Christ, we are free! We no longer have to live in the shackles of sin and under the dark cloud of God's wrath.

Oftentimes, even as Christians, we still allow ourselves to be burdened and enslaved by past sins though we have been redeemed by the ransom Christ paid for us on the cross. What past sins still bring guilt and shame to your life? Through the power and grace of God, you and I no longer have to be weighed down and imprisoned by past, present, or future sins. We must allow the gospel to remind us that, no matter how disgusting or horrific our past sins might be, the work of Christ was more than enough to wash them away. Not only are those sins completely washed away, we now have God's power to turn from and resist sin habits that keep us in bondage.

What sin is currently keeping you enslaved? Is it lust, anger, pride, pornography, gossip, self-focus, worry? We all have certain struggles that keep us from living a fully God-honoring life. However, God wants to help us turn from those sins and live with the freedom Christ's ransomed life bought for us. The work of Christ is completely sufficient. Guilt, regret, and condemnation can be completely driven away by the love and work of Christ.

In Mark 10:45, we learn more about the character of Christ. Jesus taught His disciples that the Son of Man "did not come to be served, but to serve." As we look at the cross, we should see it as Christ's defining work, a work that summarized His entire life of service. In a world where we often want to serve ourselves, Christ gives us a counter-cultural example of looking to serve the greatest needs of others. What greater way could Christ have served us than by freeing us from the captivity of our sin?

In a response of love and gratitude, we should look for practical ways to serve the people in our lives. One of the greatest ways we can serve our family and friends is to help them have a real encounter with Jesus Christ. We can respond to the gospel by looking for opportunities to point our friends and family to the saving work of Jesus Christ as we trust in the power of God to draw people to Himself. There is no greater way to serve others than by helping them receive eternal life through the ransomed life of Jesus Christ.

Jesus Christ revolutionized our lives by paying the ransom for our sin. When we put our faith in Christ, we are freed from sin's captivity and have God's power to experience a new life with Him and for Him. May this revolutionary good news propel you to glorify God in all you do: through your praise, through choosing to break away from sin, and by sharing the gospel with others.

Make It Personal

1. Where would we be without the ransom of Christ?

2. Are you living free from the guilt and regret of past sins? If not, spend time reflecting on what Christ has done for you so that you would live in the freedom that He has come to give you.

3. How can Christ's life of service propel you into living a life of serving others?

Scriptures to Read

1. Matthew 6

2. Mark 10

3. Luke 10

A Moment of Prayer

- Pray that God would help you see that Christ's life frees us from enslavement to past, present, and future sins

- Pray that you would have a greater passion to honor God by turning from the sin in your life.

- Pray that God would reveal current sins in your life so that you can confess them and draw on God's power to remove them (see 1 John 1:9).

18

Saved by God, Saved from God

Romans 5:8-10

But God shows his love for us in that while we were still sinners, Christ died for us. Since, therefore, we have now been justified by his blood, much more shall we be saved by him from the wrath of God. For if while we were enemies we were reconciled to God by the death of his Son, much more, now that we are reconciled, shall we be saved by his life.

Oftentimes, we use our Christianized jargon to talk about when we "got saved." Someone might say, "I got saved when I was a little girl," or "I got saved at summer camp." I am wondering how many of us know what we have been saved from.

What exactly have we been saved from? Is it the devil and his pitchfork? Are we saved from falling into a spiritual abyss? Or, are we saved from a boring life, and God is here to give us an exciting life? Are we saved from poverty, and God is here to give us a life of wealth and prosperity? Though some people might think God has come to save us from these things, the truth of the matter is that scripture shows us that we have actually been saved from God. Paul writes, *"Since, therefore, we have now been justified by his blood, much more shall we be saved by him from the wrath of God."* (Romans 5:9)

When we place our faith in Jesus Christ as our Savior, we actually are saved from receiving God's wrath. If we miss out on who we have been saved from, our salvation becomes extremely shallow, clichéd, and misguided. I wonder how our lives, worship, and passion for the gospel would change if, at the core of our lives, there were this deep understanding that we have been saved from God.

We've examined God's need for justice, and we've seen that Christ serves as our substitute so that we don't have to experience God's eternal judgment. I'm not sure that anyone can fully imagine what God's eternal wrath, in a place called Hell, fully looks like. However, scripture, and Jesus Christ himself, have much to say on this subject; therefore, it is important that we not drift away from this core biblical truth. If being saved from God's eternal judgment isn't a part of our theology, we will never worship God as He deserves, and we will never be the passionate followers of Christ that God calls us to be.

Why would we preach the gospel to our children if we don't believe in God's eternal punishment? Why would we share the gospel with our co-workers if there isn't a real need to be saved? I pray that you have placed your faith in Christ as your Savior, and I pray that the truth of what you have been saved from begins to shape the way you look at all of life.

I want you to imagine that you were stranded on a raft in the middle of an ocean, lost out at sea with no way of getting help. After days of being completely isolated in the vastness of the ocean, you are at last rescued by a small boat passing by.

I'm sure you would be very grateful to the people that saved you. However, wouldn't your appreciation be even greater if these boaters were able to show you what you were saved from? As you step up onto their boat, you see that under your raft were dozens of sharks sizing you up for their next meal. In the same way, understanding that we are saved from the imminent doom of God's wrath will elevate our commitment to God and motivate us to more heartfelt worship.

The irony of being saved from God is the truth that we are also being saved by God. There isn't a superhero who saves us, there isn't a megastar pastor who saves us, and there isn't a political leader who saves us. The gospel quite specifically teaches us that God saves us through Jesus Christ alone. Is Christ your Savior?

Those of us who have been saved tend to forget, or overlook, what we've been saved from. Let us allow the gospel to take root in our lives and move us to a deeper sense of worship as we reflect on the great truth that Christ has saved us from an eternity of receiving God's punishment for our transgressions.

Make It Personal

1. How does the gospel save us?

2. Why do people think that they don't need a Savior?

3. How can you live in response to the saving work of Christ?

Scriptures to Read

1. Matthew 25

2. Romans 2

3. John 15

A Moment of Prayer

- Pray that God will help you to reflect daily on what Christ has done to save you from God's eternal wrath.

- Pray that the truth of the gospel will continue to become the central force behind everything you do.

- Praise God for sending us a perfect Savior.

19

Not by Works

Galatians 2:15-16

We ourselves are Jews by birth and no Gentile sinners; yet we know that a person is not justified by works of the law but through faith in Jesus Christ, so we also have believed in Christ Jesus, in order to be justified by faith in Christ and not by works of the law, because by works of the law no one will be justified.

When I was a kid, one of the things I hated most about going to church was that I had to put on my "Sunday best." I would wake up in a bad mood on those days because I couldn't wear my basketball shorts and basketball shoes. "Hey, if God really loves me, He'll love me in my basketball shorts," I would argue. That never went over well with my parents, and it seemed like it always led to a fight on our way to church.

Though there is nothing wrong with wearing nice clothes to church, sometimes there is this unbiblical teaching that creeps into our theology that says that there are certain things we can do to get ourselves right with God. For instance: "If I just give a little more; if I just pray a little more; if I just read my Bible a little more and memorize a little more…then things will be okay between me and God." We must hold tightly to the truth of the gospel that says there is nothing we can do to be right with God, or, as the book of Galatians points out, there is nothing we can do to be "justified." Paul writes, *"yet we know that a person is not justified by works of the law but through faith in Jesus Christ."* Simply put, to be "justified" means that we are declared forgiven for our sins and seen as completely righteous in the eyes of God. Our reconciliation with God doesn't come through our efforts; it comes by faith in the efforts of Christ.

The Galatians had similar struggles as they drifted from the truth of the good news of Jesus Christ. Rather than resting in what Christ did for them, they quickly fell into misguided teaching. The Galatians were being led away from the grace of the gospel and becoming enslaved to rules and traditions.

If we get caught up in a similar lifestyle, a lifestyle based on doing works to earn salvation, we are saying that what Christ did for us, by living a perfect life and dying on the cross for our sins, wasn't enough. Do we want to look at Christ while He is on the cross and tell Him that His work isn't good enough? Christ's work is always good enough, and there is nothing we can add to what He has done. Does that mean we don't have to live a life of holiness and do good works? It actually means that we live a holy life and do good works as a response of gratitude and love towards Christ, instead of doing them as a desperate attempt to earn salvation. Christ doesn't save us because we are good; He saves us only because of His goodness, grace, and mercy.

Paul told the Galatians that we are justified by faith in Christ alone. We are not justified by our works. We are not justified by the clothes we wear, or the money we give to the church, or by that one time we served at the homeless shelter. Nothing we do justifies us before God; rather, we are justified by faith in Christ. Galatians 2:16 reminds us that we have *"believed in Christ Jesus, in order to be justified by faith in Christ and not by works of the law, because by works of the law no one will be justified."*

In order to find ourselves eternally enjoying the presence of God, we need to be justified. So, the choice we have is this: we either put faith in ourselves and our good works, or put our faith in Christ's life, death, and resurrection. Scripture assures us that when we repent of our sin and put our faith in Jesus Christ, we immediately become justified. It is our faith in Christ that justifies us, not a lifetime of good works.

Let us never drift from the truth of the gospel as the Galatians did. We do not want to hear the words that Paul wrote to them:

"I am astonished that you are so quickly deserting him who called you in the grace of Christ and are turning to a different gospel" (Galatians 1:6). As followers of Christ, our faith should be in Him rather than in any good works we do. God does want the Christian life to be marked by good works, but we must never believe the lie that our good works are going to save us.

Make It Personal

1. How do we, at times, try to earn our salvation through good works?

2. Why won't good works save us?

3. Would you rather do good works as a response to being loved, or out of a fear in hopes of avoiding God's punishment? Why?

Scriptures to Read

1. Galatians 1

2. Galatians 2

3. Romans 12

A Moment of Prayer

- Pray that God will help you to see Christ's work on the cross as completely sufficient.

- Pray that God will continue to remind you that it is only through faith in Christ that you are justified.

- Pray that you would never drift from the glorious truths of the gospel.

20

Finding Peace in God

Colossians 1:19-22

*For in him all the fullness of God was pleased to dwell, and
through him to reconcile to himself all things, whether on earth
or in heaven, making peace by the blood of his cross. And you,
who once were alienated and hostile in mind, doing evil deeds,
he has now reconciled in his body of flesh by his death, in order to
present you holy and blameless and above reproach before him.*

In a world gone crazy, it seems that people will do anything
to find a quick, easy way to experience peace in their life. We
find ourselves stressed by family, work, school, relationships, and
finances. These areas of our lives seem to fluctuate continuously
and the reality is that they always will. With this much chaos in
our lives, we are always looking for the next best thing to offer
serenity. Whether you are pursuing the "Self Help" section of
your local book store or doing Internet searches for the "Top Ten
Stress Relievers," we can all admit that we are seeking ways to
experience more peace here on earth. However, we must understand that peace with God is absolutely necessary before we can
experience peace here in this world.

As we examine Colossians 1:19–22, we see that our sin causes
our relationship with God to be marred. Rather than being uni-
fied with God, we are alienated from God. How can we experience real and everlasting peace when we are alienated from our
God?

As we have learned throughout this book, our sin is the only
reason for our alienation from God. It is our "evil deeds" and
"hostile mind" that cause the division that exists between us and
God, as Paul writes in Colossians. Trying to experience peace

in this world is an absolutely pointless endeavor until we come to a place of peace with God where our sin is no longer causing hostility between us and God. We may achieve fleeting moments of peace, but everlasting peace comes only through Jesus Christ.

God wants us to experience peace in this world, but hopefully we will see that peace in this world can't be experienced until we are at peace with God. Paul writes in Philippians 4:7 that the peace of God *"surpasses all understanding."* That is the kind of peace God wants us to experience, a peace that can come only through Christ and will surpass anything we can imagine.

We don't need to be stressed, worried, or anxious. God wants us to live with an undeniable peace that comes from Him. As followers of Jesus Christ, we can be the ones who live with an indescribable peace that the world hungers for. Oftentimes, however, our lives don't seem any more peaceful than others.

We can experience God's peace in this world gone crazy only to the extent that we stay connected every day to the power of the gospel message. We will never experience peace here on this earth if we turn our backs on, or forget, what Christ has done to bring peace between us and God. Satan would love for us to get so caught up in the chaos of this world that we forget to reflect on what Christ has done for us on the cross. Let us be people who anticipate receiving God's peace as we grow closer to what Christ did to bring us forgiveness, peace, and salvation.

Make It Personal

1. Are you currently at peace with God? Have you repented of your sin and placed your faith fully in Christ? If you want to put your faith in Jesus and receive God's peace, turn to page 199 for guidance.

2. Have you taken the time to rejoice in the truth that you and others are completely reconciled to God?

3. How can you stay connected to Christ and the gospel so that you can live with the peace of God each and every day?

Scriptures to Read

1. Romans 5

2. Philippians 4

3. 2 Corinthians 5:11–21

A Moment of Prayer

- Ask God to reveal to you where stress, worry, and anxiety are plaguing your life.

- Pray that you would come to understand that everlasting peace only comes through Christ.

- Pray for those people in your life who aren't at peace with God and who need to embrace the gospel of Jesus Christ.

21

Dwelling with God

Revelation 21:3

*And I heard a loud voice from the throne saying,
"Behold, the dwelling place of God is with man. He
will dwell with them, and they will be his people, and
God himself will be with them as their God."*

In the early chapters of the Bible we get a pristine picture of God dwelling with man in the Garden of Eden. That reality is quickly destroyed, however, as both Adam and Eve are cast from the Garden and from God's presence because of their sin. But at the end of the Bible, the picture we see in Revelation 21 is of a fully restored and eternal relationship between man and God.

In Revelation 21:3, the apostle John writes that *"the dwelling place of God is with man"* and that *"He will dwell with them, and they will be his people."* We can look forward to an amazing future, a time when nothing will inhibit us from dwelling with God. However, an eternity with God comes only through Jesus Christ. It is Jesus who taught, *"I am the way, and the truth, and the life. No one comes to the Father except through me"* (John 14:6).

We have learned in previous chapters that it is only through the work of Christ on the cross that you and I can find forgiveness of sin and become reconciled to God. And as we examine Revelation 21:3, I think we uncover the greatest blessing of the gospel, which is an earthly and eternal relationship with God.

Oftentimes we selfishly approach God wanting to receive benefits that will make our lives better. We seek God in hope that He will make our marriages better, our careers more successful, and our children better behaved. And though God has the power to influence all these aspects of our life, we shouldn't pursue Him for these reasons. Instead, we should be blown away by, and fully satisfied with, the greatest benefit of the gospel—knowing and being with God. Although on this side of eternity we can experience only a portion of this relationship, we should be amazed that we can know God at all, and look forward to a day when we will know and dwell with more Him fully.

Pastor John Piper writes, "The gospel of Christ proclaims the news that he has purchased by his death ten thousand blessings for his bride. But none of these gifts will lead to final joy if they have not first led to God. And not one gospel blessing will be enjoyed by anyone for whom the gospel's greatest gift was not the Lord himself."

The gift of the gospel is God. Is the Lord the greatest gift of your life? Do you cherish the gospel because you cherish your relationship with God? I know that it is easier for me to focus my attention on the blessings that make my life better than to focus on the ultimate blessing of having a relationship with God. In the midst of our families, careers, vacations, financial troubles, soccer games, and birthday parties, God wants us to become totally consumed with Him. When we become consumed with God, He becomes our greatest, joy, treasure, and priority.

A couple of years ago, my parents and my wife's parents helped us to buy a house. Not many young couples are able to buy a house in the crazy housing market of California. Though this is an amazing blessing, I don't believe for one second that our parents want us to fall completely in love with the house and neglect our relationship with them. They want us to enjoy the blessing of the house, but they don't want it to blind us from seeing the true gift; the gift of having loving parents. To take the love we have for our parents and give it to the house would be insulting.

In the same way, God doesn't want us to become so consumed by the blessings we receive from our relationship with Him that we neglect the most important relationship possible. I confess that there are times when I do neglect my relationship with the Lord, and I imagine that there is nothing more hurtful to God than to see His child live a self-focused life rather than a God-focused life. Let us repent of the times in our lives when knowing God isn't our highest priority and greatest joy.

By no means do I want us to be people who ignore the countless blessings we receive once we fully trust in the finished work of Christ. However, our greatest desire should be for our greatest blessing—knowing God. Heaven is going to be a place where we get to dwell in the presence of God, but don't wait until then for Him to become your greatest joy, your greatest treasure, and your greatest blessing.

Make It Personal

1. What is keeping you from enjoying the blessings of being in a relationship with God?

2. Do you focus more on God's material blessings, or on the blessing of God dwelling in you? What differences will your focus make to your sense of peace and joy?

3. How can you begin to live a God-focused life today?

Scriptures to Read

1. Matthew 1

2. Leviticus 26

3. Psalm 26

A Moment of Prayer

- Pray that having the presence of God will become more important to you than having the presents of God.

- Pray that you would live for Him, not for yourself. Confess the times in your life when knowing God wasn't your priority.

- Pray that God would help you to truly look forward to an eternity with Him.

22

Raised with Christ

Romans 6:5–11

For if we have been united with him in a death like his, we shall certainly be united with him in a resurrection like his. We know that our old self was crucified with him in order that the body of sin might be brought to nothing, so that we would no longer be enslaved to sin. For one who has died has been set free from sin. Now if we have died with Christ, we believe that we will also live with him. We know that Christ, being raised from the dead, will never die again; death no longer has dominion over him. For the death he died he died to sin, once for all, but the life he lives he lives to God. So you also must consider yourselves dead to sin and alive to God in Christ Jesus.

Meditating on the cross means that we also get to mediate on the resurrection. If we fail to look at the cross, we'll miss out on what Christ accomplished, but if we fail to look at the resurrection, we'll miss out on the power we have to live a completely new life. The resurrection is so vital to our faith that Paul writes, *"If Christ has not been raised, then our preaching is in vain and your faith is in vain"* (1 Corinthians 15:14). A couple of verses later he writes, more emphatically, *"And if Christ has not been raised, your faith is futile and you are still in your sins"* (1 Corinthians 15:17).

If Jesus failed to rise from the dead, it would mean that He also failed to accomplish anything on the cross. However, the resurrection gives us confidence that Christ's work on the cross did succeed in taking away the sins of those who fully trust in Him. The resurrection of Jesus was God's validation of Christ's redeeming work on the cross.

Because of our sin, we are cursed. Our sin separates us from

God and, as a result, we will receive everlasting punishment—an eternal spiritual death apart from God. The gospel message tells us, however, that after spending three days in the tomb, Jesus Christ rose from the dead, showing that He fully conquered the effects of the curse. Now, as a result, we have the potential to receive the blessings of the gospel rather than punishment for our sin. Jesus' resurrection testifies that the curse of sin is abolished for those who choose to place their trust in the life, death, and resurrection of Jesus Christ.

The resurrection isn't something that only Jesus experiences. After placing our faith in Christ, we also will experience the resurrection. Our faith in Christ connects us with Christ's death and His resurrection. Through His death, our old life is crucified and we are declared completely forgiven. Paul writes, *"We know that our old self was crucified with him in order that the body of sin might be brought to nothing, so that we would no longer be enslaved to sin"* (Romans 6:6). Now that we are freed from sin through Christ's death, we are resurrected to a brand new life here on earth.

In our new life in Christ, we can put to death sin and daily be concerned about living for God's glory. You now have the amazing opportunity and privilege to live a life that brings God honor by the way you dress, speak, treat others, serve others, engage with non-believers, show compassion, spend money, etc. Everything we do, through the power of this new life that we have in Christ, can be a life dedicated to the glory of God. Paul writes, *"So, whether you eat or drink, or whatever you do, do all to the glory of God"* (1 Corinthians 10:31).

In our old life we had no desire or potential to honor God, but now, as one of the blessings of our salvation, we are resurrected and have resurrection power to live a new life that pleases God. Are you embracing this new life, or are you falling back into old temptations? When we fail to recognize the power the resurrection gives to our life, we will find ourselves slowly drifting back to a life that looks like the old one rather than the new one.

The new life that God's resurrection power gives us here on Earth also points us to our future resurrection, when we will be with God for all eternity in a new heaven and a new earth. With the effects of the curse fully lifted, we look forward in hope to the day when we will be given a new body and be fully reconciled to God.

Christ's resurrection from the dead demonstrates the power of God. With that same power, we can be raised to a new life here on earth and eventually to a new life with God in heaven for all eternity. Let us rejoice in the undeserved opportunity we have to say goodbye to our old life and hello to a new life in Jesus Christ.

Make It Personal

1. If you believe in the resurrection, and you believe that your faith in Jesus connects you to His resurrection, what difference will that make in your life?

2. What happens if we reflect on the cross but not on the resurrection? What happens if we reflect on the resurrection but not on the cross?

3. What in your life looks more like your old life than your new life? What can you do to live in your resurrected life?

Scriptures to Read

1. Galatians 3

2. 1 Corinthians 15

3. Romans 6

A Moment of Prayer

- Praise God that He has raised you to a brand-new life.

- Pray that you would depend on the power of God to live a brand-new life.

- Pray that God would awaken your heart to all aspects of the gospel.

Section Four

A Faithful Response to the Gospel

The gospel demands a clear and specific response. If we want to enjoy the pleasures of being reconciled to God and the blessings that come with the gospel, then we must make sure we are responding faithfully.

Colossians 3:1–17

If then you have been raised with Christ, seek the things that are above, where Christ is, seated at the right hand of God. Set your minds on things that are above, not on things that are on earth. For you have died, and your life is hidden with Christ in God. When Christ who is your life appears, then you also will appear with him in glory.

Put to death therefore what is earthly in you: sexual immorality, impurity, passion, evil desire, and covetousness, which is idolatry. On account of these the wrath of God is coming. In these you too once walked, when you were living in them. But now you must put them all away: anger, wrath, malice, slander, and obscene talk from your mouth. Do not lie to one another, seeing that you have put off the old self with its practices and have put on the new self, which is being renewed in knowledge after the image of its creator. Here there is not Greek and Jew, circumcised and uncircumcised, barbarian, Scythian, slave, free; but Christ is all, and in all.

Put on then, as God's chosen ones, holy and beloved, compassionate hearts, kindness, humility, meekness, and patience, bearing with one another and, if one has a complaint against another, forgiving each other; as the Lord has forgiven you, so you also must forgive. And above all these put on love, which binds everything together in perfect harmony. And let the peace of Christ rule in your hearts, to which indeed you were called in one body. And be thankful. Let the word of Christ dwell in you richly, teaching and admonishing one another in all wisdom, singing psalms and hymns and spiritual songs, with thankfulness in your hearts to God. And whatever you do, in word or deed, do everything in the name of the Lord Jesus, giving thanks to God the Father through him.

23

Faith in Christ

Galatians 3:10-14

For all who rely on works of the law are under a curse; for it is written, "Cursed be everyone who does not abide by all things written in the Book of the Law, and do them." Now it is evident that no one is justified before God by the law, for "The righteous shall live by faith." But the law is not of faith, rather "The one who does them shall live by them." Christ redeemed us from the curse of the law by becoming a curse for us—for it is written, "Cursed is everyone who is hanged on a tree"—so that in Christ Jesus the blessing of Abraham might come to the Gentiles, so that we might receive the promised Spirit through faith.

Our eternal destination is totally determined by our faith. Some may have faith in their good deeds and, based on those deeds, trust they will receive eternal life. Others may place their faith on the belief that there is no God and that when you die it's over, and your body will just decompose in the grave. We all have faith in something. The Christian, though, by definition is someone who has faith in nothing other than the God-Man Jesus Christ and, more specifically, His life, death, and resurrection.

Faith is having the knowledge and conviction that the Bible is true and its testimony of the life, death, and resurrection of Christ is the only way to be reconciled eternally to God. Do you have that knowledge of the gospel? Do you believe the gospel with a strong conviction? Is your faith in the finished work of Jesus Christ?

The gospel message demands that we make a response of faith to the finished work of Jesus Christ. If a person wants to inherit the promises and blessings of a restored relationship with God, then a faith in Christ is essential. For the seasoned believer, faith in Christ isn't a one-time act. Faith continues every day. In fact, if you want to continue to mature, bring glory to God, and live a truly abundant life, it is possible only as your faith grows in our loving and sovereign God.

The truth of scripture is that we will either, through faith in Christ, receive the undeserved blessing of eternal life or, without faith in Christ, receive our deserved punishment. Our deserved eternal punishment is what Galatians 3:10–14 refers to as the "curse." Because we all have fallen short of God's standards, we live under the curse of death and eternal condemnation.

The good news of the gospel, however, is that God, in His love, provides a way to remove the curse. Paul writes, *"Christ redeemed us from the curse of the law by becoming a curse for us."* God doesn't arbitrarily lift the curse, because that would go completely against His character of being just. Instead, God sends a substitute, Jesus Christ, to be our curse. God's love and justice meet at the cross. It is there that He can both punish sin and rescue His people from their fatal punishment.

The back story to the book of Galatians is that there were false teachers who were confusing early believers by teaching them that they needed more than faith to be saved. To truly find salvation, they claimed, there were certain additional rituals that had to also be completed. The gospel says emphatically that all we need for salvation is faith in what Christ has done and that we are not to place faith in any attempts to earn a reconciled relationship with God through our own efforts.

The benefits of eternal life—which include receiving the Holy Spirit, forgiveness of sins, adoption into God's family, joy, peace and purpose—are all given to us when we place our faith in God's salvation plan. God wants us to humble ourselves by recognizing our sin and our need for a Savior, and then to place our faith in Him and in what He has done to reconcile us to Himself. As we continue to grow in the gospel, we must understand that our faith must be in the life, death, and resurrection of Jesus Christ. A vague faith that there is a God out there somewhere, or that God is love, is not enough. Our faith must be in the truth that Jesus Christ is God who became man and that His life, death, and resurrection are completely sufficient to forgive our sins and redeem us to a relationship with God.

Many of us can agree on the necessity of faith. However, at times we, like the Galatians, get confused and live as if we are actually saved by our good works. We run around living completely insane lives trying to impress others—and God—by how many Bible studies we can attend and how many hours we can serve at our local church.

When was the last time you rested and rejoiced in the finished work of Christ? There's no doubt that our faith should be accompanied by good works, but we should also rest in the truth that nothing we do adds to our salvation. When we try to earn our salvation, it's as if we are standing before God saying that what Christ did for us on the cross wasn't good enough.

Every day, as you reflect on the gospel and are reminded of your sin, continue to place your faith in Christ alone. Respond to His love by trusting Him as your Lord and King, with every detail of your life.

Make It Personal

1. Is your faith in Christ growing daily as you trust Him with your salvation? How is your trust in Christ being seen in the way you live your daily life?

2. Why is faith in Christ alone our only hope for salvation?

3. What area of your life do you need to hand over to God in faith?

Scriptures to Read

1. Galatians 3

2. John 4

3. 1 Peter 5

A Moment of Prayer

- Pray that God would open your eyes to see the absolute necessity of faith in Christ.

- Pray that God would reveal to you where you are trying to earn your relationship with Him based on your works.

- Pray that more and more people in your church would become passionate about the good news of the gospel.

24

Gospel Repentance

Acts 3:18-20

"But what God foretold by the mouth of all the prophets, that his Christ would suffer, he thus fulfilled. Repent, therefore, and turn again, that your sins may be blotted out, that times of refreshing may come from the presence of the Lord, and that he may send the Christ appointed for you, Jesus."

The gospel demands a response. If we have a real encounter with Jesus Christ, there will be evidence of a changed life. For example, I can tell everyone that I am working out five times a week, eating healthy, and losing weight, but if people don't see any changes in my body they'll know it's not true because there's no evidence. In the same way, we can tell everyone that we are walking with Christ, but if there are no real changes in our life no one will believe us.

One of the first responses that the gospel demands from us is repentance. If we have genuinely put our faith in Jesus, the evidence will be seen in our repentance. Repentance and faith always go together. In Peter's famous sermon in Acts 3, he says, *"Repent, therefore, and turn again, that your sins may be blotted out."* Repentance means making a deliberate effort to turn away from our lifestyle of sin. Rather than pursuing sin, we must turn in the complete opposite direction and pursue God and the life that God intended for us, a life of holiness, obedience and righteousness.

However, before we can turn and start pursuing God, we must first acknowledge that we are headed in the wrong direction. The Bible calls this acknowledgement of sin "confession." Confession and repentance are connected to each other. Without repentance, our confession isn't genuine and truly remorseful, and without genuine confession there's nothing to repent from.

In Psalm 32, David writes of the impact of confessed and unconfessed sin:

"Blessed is the one whose transgression is forgiven, whose sin is covered.

Blessed is the man against whom the LORD counts no iniquity, and in whose spirit there is no deceit.

For when I kept silent, my bones wasted away through my groaning all day long.

For day and night your hand was heavy upon me; my strength was dried up as by the heat of summer.

I acknowledged my sin to you, and I did not cover my iniquity;

I said, "I will confess my transgressions to the LORD," and you forgave the iniquity of my sin."   (Psalm 32:1–5)

Repentance means that we stop and admit that we've gone the wrong direction and that our life choices are deliberate acts of rebellion towards God. To admit that we have sinned against God takes humility, but, until we take this step, we will never recognize our need for forgiveness and our need for a Savior. If we fail to recognize our need, we will never ask for, or receive, God's forgiveness.

For those of you who have yet to put your faith in Jesus, what's keeping you from admitting that you have a sin problem and need a Savior? What's keeping you from turning from your current life and towards Christ?

To my brothers and sisters in Christ, we must understand that repentance must become a daily activity that we incorporate into our lives. Daily we mourn our sins, confess them before God, and rejoice in the truth that Christ has shed His blood for our forgiveness. Then, before God, we commit ourselves to turning away from those sins, and we rely on His grace and the power of the Holy Spirit to give us the strength we need to grow into a life of godliness.

The good news of the gospel is that times of "refreshing" are promised when we fall on our knees in repentance and turn, by the power of God, towards Him rather than towards sinful and selfish desires. I pray that we would be people of humility and recognize our desperate need for the strength of our Savior.

Make It Personal

1. Why are we often so prideful when it comes to admitting we are wrong?

2. Why is repentance necessary to receive the blessings of the gospel? Why is it an evidence of faith?

3. What can you do to make repentance a daily activity in your life?

Scriptures to Read

1. Nehemiah 1

2. 1 John 1

3. Psalm 32

A Moment of Prayer

- Pray that you would be humble enough to daily confess and repent of your sin.

- Pray that God will reveal to you the sins that are harming your relationship with Him and need to be confessed.

- Praise God for always being willing to forgive us of our sins.

25

Radical Commitment

Luke 9:57–62

*As they were going along the road, someone said to him, "I will
follow you wherever you go." And Jesus said to him, "Foxes
have holes, and birds of the air have nests, but the Son of Man
has nowhere to lay his head." To another he said, "Follow me."
But he said, "Lord, let me first go and bury my father." And
Jesus said to him, "Leave the dead to bury their own dead. But
as for you, go and proclaim the kingdom of God." Yet another
said, "I will follow you, Lord, but let me first say farewell to
those at my home." Jesus said to him, "No one who puts his hand
to the plow and looks back is fit for the kingdom of God."*

The gospel is radical, and Jesus is looking for a radical commitment from people who are being transformed by His saving
grace. In Luke 9:57–62, we see Jesus teaching us about radical
discipleship. In this passage, there are three men who had the
opportunity to literally follow the Messiah. But before they
decide to follow Him, Jesus wants to make sure they fully understand what it means to be a disciple. We must let what Jesus says
to these men shape our understanding of what it means to live as
a disciple of Christ.

In the first interaction, Jesus responds to the bold claims of
a man who says, "I will follow you wherever you go." This is an
attitude that Jesus wants us to have, but as we examine Jesus'
response, we see that Jesus wants to make sure this would-be
disciple truly understands the commitment he is making. Do we
really want to follow Jesus wherever He goes? Jesus, the King of
Kings, didn't come to live in a king's palace. Instead, Jesus had
"nowhere to lay his head." This highlights to us that the life of

Jesus wasn't marked by ease and comfort. If we truly want to follow Him, we have to understand that a life of discipleship will not always be easy and comfortable.

Jesus was committed to walking the road to Jerusalem, where He would carry His own cross and die an excruciating death for the sins of others. Like Jesus, whom we are following, we will not have a life free of pain, suffering, or even persecution. Jesus is looking for people like you and me who are willing to go and do whatever He wants. Are you willing to follow Jesus wherever He goes?

In the second interaction we see someone who wants to take the time to go and bury his father, which seems like a reasonable request. However, the Jewish process for burying a loved one could take up to a year. Jesus knew that this man was making an excuse in order to dodge the calling of faithfully following Him. This would-be disciple was trying to look committed without actually being committed. What excuses do you give Jesus when it comes to living for Him and His mission? Are you too busy? Is your job more important? Is your college education keeping you from living fully for Christ?

We have already seen that Jesus came on a mission to save sinners and reconcile them to the Father. However, His mission isn't complete. He has empowered us to partner with Him to continue His mission here on Earth by sharing the gospel message with others. Though we may have plenty of excuses, Jesus says to us, "But as for you, go and proclaim the kingdom of God." This isn't an option; this is a lifestyle for all believers.

The would-be disciple we see in the third interaction also expresses his desire to follow Jesus, but first he wants to say farewell to those at his home. Drawing upon the agricultural imagery of his day, Jesus responds by saying, "No one who puts his hand to the plow and looks back is fit for the kingdom of God." Plowing while looking back inevitably takes you off course. This can have a devastating effect on a farmer's crop. Likewise, to look back after committing yourself to following Jesus is devastating to your life with Christ and to the impact Christ wants you to have in the world as His disciple. Therefore, following Jesus means that we must have an undying focus on Him.

If we are to be disciples of Jesus, we must focus on Him and His Kingdom work. If we keep looking back, we aren't faithful disciples. A plowman who keeps looking back will have a messed-up crop, and if we keep looking in other directions and fail to focus on Christ, we will have a messed-up Christian life.

The aim of this book is to help us understand and fall more in love with the truth of the gospel. As God awakens us to the joy of the gospel and the joy of knowing Him, hopefully we will see how the gospel impacts every aspect of our lives. As the gospel begins to shape everything about us, I pray that we will begin to understand that our response to the good news must be a radical commitment to following Jesus and His mission of advancing the gospel.

Make It Personal

1. What excuses do you love to give God when it comes to following Him wherever He wants you to go?

2. How do we find the courage to answer God's call to be radical disciples?

3. What is God calling you to do today to advance His mission here on Earth?

Scriptures to Read

1. Matthew 4

2. Matthew 7

3. Luke 9

A Moment of Prayer

- Pray that God would give you the courage to answer His daily call to a radical commitment to Him and His mission.

- Pray that you would see more clearly what God is specifically calling you to do as His follower.

- Praise God that He views you as worthy of being used by Him to make an eternal impact in the lives of others.

26

Life Is Worship

Romans 12:1

I appeal to you therefore, brothers, by the mercies of God, to present your bodies as a living sacrifice, holy and acceptable to God, which is your spiritual worship.

Often, our Christian walk seems like a high speed rollercoaster, constantly going up and down, with extreme highs and lows. One of the primary reasons we live on a spiritual rollercoaster is that we often base our relationship with God on circumstances. If things are going well—if we have money in the bank account, food in the refrigerator, a boyfriend or a girlfriend, and gas in the car—then our relationship with God is amazing. However, if life isn't going according to our "Ten Year Plan," our relationship with God suffers. When we go through ups and downs, our worship of God can be compromised. Instead of living in constant and consistent worship for the glory of God, we can be controlled by our sometimes uncontrollable circumstances.

Romans 12:1 is one of the most important verses in the New Testament. It accurately and succinctly summarizes how we are to respond to the gospel. Paul challenges us "to present (our) bodies as a living sacrifice, holy and acceptable God." If our relationships with God are even mildly based on our circumstances, our worship of God will not be as passionate, authentic, and consistent as God deserves and desires.

When Romans 12:1 mentions the "mercies of God" it points the Christian to the source of our worship: it is not our circumstances, but God's grace and mercy seen through Jesus Christ. It is only as we stay connected to the life-sustaining power of the gospel that we will be able to worship God with all our life as He deserves.

We are like laptop batteries. On our best days we can only run for a couple hours before needing to be recharged. If a laptop isn't reconnected to its power source, it is completely worthless. It may have the largest hard drive, fastest processors, and coolest features, but without power it may as well be thrown away. Similarly, if we don't stay connected to the reality of the gospel, we will never be willing to "present (our) bodies as a living sacrifice, holy and acceptable to God." Instead, our worship will be half-hearted and uninspired.

When we stay connected to the gospel, its life-changing message of God's grace will move us to worship God. There may be tragedy in our life, confusion about our future, or devastation in our world, but God's love and mercy, seen in what Christ did on the cross to rescue us from our eternal demise, will bring us to the throne of worship. In other words, if we stay aware of the gospel message, we should never have an excuse not to worship Him wholeheartedly.

There are times when it is easy for us to get passionate about worship—when the music is played professionally, when the lights set the mood, and when we are just "feeling it." However, God wants us to see our entire life as an opportunity to bring Him praise. God does enjoy our jubilant songs, our shouts of joy, and our prayers of thankfulness, but He also wants an entire life that that is concerned with honoring Him.

Our worship should be this all-consuming life endeavor, not something that is compartmentalized, not something based on a specific time or location, and definitely not something based on whether or not we are having a good day. Our every breath, word, action, and thought has the potential to bring either worship or displeasure to God. This means that the way we treat our spouses has the potential to be an act of worship to God. The way we dress and the way we treat our bodies have potential to be acts of worship to God. The way we deal with our finances and the way we spend our time also have potential to be acts of worship to God.

All of life should be worship. But to have that kind of focus and motivation means that we will need to stay centered on the amazing truths of God's mercies seen through Jesus Christ. My prayer is that these devotionals have been helping you stay centered on the foundational truths of the gospel and that God is starting to awaken you towards living a life fully devoted to worshiping Him.

Make It Personal

1. Why should we be concerned with worshiping God?

2. What happens if worship is only singing songs on Sunday morning?

3. How can your life be more of a source of worship to God? What can you do to "present your body as a living sacrifice, holy and acceptable to God?"

Scriptures to Read

1. Psalm 29

2. Romans 12

3. Colossians 3

A Moment of Prayer

- Pray that you would become a passionate worshiper of God.

- Pray that your worship will not be determined by your circumstances.

- Pray that God will show you ways in which your entire life can become an act of worship to Him.

27

Pursuing Righteousness

1 Peter 2:24–25

He himself bore our sins in his body on the tree, that we might die to sin and live to righteousness. By his wounds you have been healed. For you were straying like sheep, but have now returned to the Shepherd and Overseer of your souls.

I'm kind of an emotional guy; especially on Sunday evenings at 8 p.m. while watching *Extreme Makeover: Home Edition*. My wife, Kari, is always making fun of me because usually within the first five minutes of the show I'm already shedding a few tears. I love seeing how the *Extreme Makeover* crew gives struggling families a helping hand by completely transforming their living situations. Their houses often go from being almost unlivable to homes that can be featured in magazines for the rich and famous.

Extreme Makeover is a good analogy of how the gospel transforms our lives. Just like these houses go through complete renovations, we should look completely different when Jesus becomes the center of our lives. Ask yourself this question: Has God done an extreme makeover in my life since the time I placed my faith in Christ? What is the evidence?

1 Peter 2:24–25 points us straight to the cross as it refers to Jesus Christ bearing our sins "on the tree." As this scripture continues, we see that God has an expectation that we will continue to die to sin and live a life of righteousness. A life of righteousness is a life concerned with honoring and glorifying God. As we think about righteousness, it's not surprising that Jesus is our perfect example. It is only because of Jesus' perfectly righteous life that He was able to be our atoning sacrifice. This is the life we need to be committed to. A life of righteousness doesn't mean

that we will never struggle with sin. However, a person who has been transformed by the gospel will be a person who is passionate about living a brand-new life.

Too often our churches are filled with people who say they have made commitments to following Christ, but have lives that look no different from those of people who are living for the world. Something is wrong. We can, and should, expect some clear distinctions between someone who is living for Christ and someone who is not.

The good news of the gospel is that, no matter who we are or what we've done, by the power of the cross we can be completely healed—not necessarily healed in a physical sense, but completely healed in the spiritual sense. When we can truly grasp what it means to be healed from our disease of sin, we will be moved to passionately honor the One who has provided us the cure.

Our cure is Jesus Christ and the way we honor Him is to live a new life of holiness. In those areas where we once lived for ourselves, we now live for God. In those areas where we were once governed by the world's way of thinking, we are now led by the Spirit. *"For the love of Christ controls us, because we have concluded this: that one has died for all, therefore all have died; and he died for all, that those who live might no longer live for themselves but for him who for their sake died and was raised"* (2 Corinthians 5:14–15).

The Bible calls this process of leaving sin and running towards righteousness "sanctification". We may get discouraged at times by the ups and downs of our struggle with sin, but we can have confidence knowing that, through the Holy Spirit, God is empowering us in this sanctifying process.

I know that as I continue to fall more in love with Christ and what He did for me, I am motivated more than ever to faithfully fight sins like anger and pride. Though the battle is constant, living within the shadow of God's forgiveness gives me the strength and the desire to abandon these sins, be transformed by God, and experience a life filled with the Fruit of the Spirit (see

Galatians 5). It is only by the power of the Holy Spirit and the grace of God that we can move towards a righteous life.

As you examine the saving work of Jesus Christ, it is extremely important to also examine whether or not you are fully committed to living a new life in Christ. When you became a Christian, did you just pray a prayer of salvation and then never think about it again? Or did the living God open your heart and mind to truly receive Jesus Christ as your Lord and Savior? How can you tell? I suggest that you examine whether or not you are fully committed to living a transformed life.

When we truly embrace the gospel message and put our faith in the perfectly righteous Jesus, He will revolutionize our lives by giving us a distaste for sin and a sweet taste for holiness. This new life will bring Him great glory and honor, and bring us great freedom.

Make It Personal

1. Are you allowing God to do a complete makeover in your life right now?

2. In what area of your life are you resisting the makeover God wants to do?

3. How can you live a life that is committed to pursuing righteousness and holiness?

Scriptures to Read

1. Exodus 15

2. 1 Peter 1

3. 1 Peter 2

A Moment of Prayer

• Pray that God will help you become more and more like Christ and that you will have the desire to cooperate.

• Pray that God would surround you with people who will help you grow in your ability to live out your faith.

• Praise God for being faithful to you even when you are unfaithful to Him.

28

Mourning Sin

Matthew 5:4

"Blessed are those who mourn, for they shall be comforted."

In what is seen as Jesus' most famous sermon, the Sermon on the Mount, He starts off with the greatly familiar, but often overlooked, "Beatitudes." These beatitudes, or blessings, come with accompanying commands, and these commands can turn us towards a more authentic discipleship. As we look at one specific beatitude, Matthew 5:4, Jesus reminds us of a blessing that comes to us when we mourn. But why are we called to mourn?

In the context of the Beatitudes, the mourning Jesus is talking about has to do with being deeply aware of, and emotionally moved by, the sin that corrupts our lives. Theologian and pastor Martyn Lloyd Jones says, "a man who truly faces himself, and examines himself and his life, is a man who must of necessity mourn for his sins."

Hopefully, we've already come to a place where we've recognized that we have been deeply disobedient to God, and have responded by putting our faith in Jesus as our Savior. However, to be growing Christians, we must do more than deal with our sin at the moment when we put our faith in Jesus Christ.

How aware are you of your daily sin? Do you hate your sin? Do you mourn over the damage it is doing to your relationship with God? Do you sweep your sin under a carpet and move on with your life?

What we see in the Beatitudes is that Jesus Christ has promised us blessing when we mourn our sin. To mourn over our sin means to be deeply aware of how our sin impacts our lives and our relationship with God. It means we are convicted by our disobedience and have a deep desire to turn away from our sin and honor God.

Living a life of mourning doesn't seem to fit with the teaching in scripture to live with constant joy (Galatians 5:22–23). However, this teaching on mourning doesn't mean we walk around with gloomy faces. Yes, we should be convicted by the hurt we cause God and ourselves through our sin, but the more aware we are of our sin, the more aware we are of God's grace. As we are reminded of God's grace, we experience the blessing of the great, deep, and wide love that God has for us. Our mourning leads to blessing because it reminds us of God's fantastic free gift of forgiveness and new life.

As the gospel becomes more central to my life, I am becoming more aware of the sins that plague my life. When I paid little attention to the gospel and kept it in the background of my life, I barely noticed my sin. Sure, I may have felt guilty every once in awhile, but I wasn't concerned about how my sin impacted me or, more importantly, how it impacted my relationship with a holy God. However, when God brought the gospel to the forefront of my life, its great news made me intensely aware of my sin that sent Jesus to the cross.

If we don't mourn our sin, I believe that it is because we have lost our awareness of what Christ did to bring us into a reconciled relationship with God. Paul said it this way: *"The saying is trustworthy and deserving of full acceptance, that Christ Jesus came into the world to save sinners, of whom I am the foremost"* (1 Timothy 1:15). Paul knew his past, he knew his sin, and he knew what Christ did to save him. This awareness shaped the life of Paul, and it should shape the lives of all who call on the name of Jesus. Jesus isn't concerned about building up the self-esteem of the world. Instead, Jesus tells us to pay special attention to our failures, because they impact us at the core of who we are.

Let us be people who mourn because we understand the pain our sin brings to God as well as the destruction it brings to our lives. Then let us also rejoice, knowing that when our mourning moves us to *"confess our sins, he is faithful and just to forgive us our sins and to cleanse us from all unrighteousness"* (1 John 1:9).

Make It Personal

1. How can you mourn over your sin on a daily basis?

2. How can this discipline bring you to a deeper awareness of the gospel?

3. Do you mourn over your sin? What sins in your life do you ignore or pay little attention to?

Scriptures to Read

1. Matthew 5

2. 1 Corinthians 5

3. Nehemiah 1

A Moment of Prayer

- Pray that God would help you to not take sin lightly and that you would sense how it makes God feel when you sin.

- Confess your sins in prayer by praying something like: "God, I did _____. I renounce it as wrong and commit myself to turning away from it and towards You."

- Praise God for always being willing to forgive your sin.

29

Mature in Christ

Colossians 1:28

*Him we proclaim, warning everyone and teaching everyone with
all wisdom, that we may present everyone mature in Christ.*

Paul was clearly passionate about proclaiming the gospel of
Jesus Christ. But Paul was also passionate about helping people
become mature followers of Christ. As we become people who
are falling more in love with Christ and more in love with the
gospel truths, we must have an equal passion to continue growing in all aspects of our faith.

It is easy to raise your hand to accept Christ at a local church
service, or to pray a prayer asking Christ to come into your heart,
but it is a lot more difficult to live out your faith every day. In fact,
our "professions" of faith in Christ may mean absolutely nothing
if it's not impacting our lives daily.

We can spend years "playing the game" of being a Christian
and never see steady growth towards Christ-likeness. If we only
make a one-time response to the gospel, and then go on living
the same way we have our entire lives, the gospel hasn't really
changed us, and we haven't truly surrendered our life to Christ.
When we make an authentic response to the gospel, we will
begin a lifelong journey of living lives that are more and more
honoring to God.

This journey towards Christ-likeness shows us how the gospel
impacts our marriages, families, careers, finances, and every other
aspect of life. As the gospel becomes more central to our lives,
we should see it directly correlate to the way we love and serve

our spouses. As the gospel becomes the defining truth of our lives, it should impact our sexual purity and desire to honor God with our bodies. As we fall more in love with Christ, it should transform how we spend and invest our money. When the gospel saturates every aspect of our lives, it has the power to transform us into the type of people God desires us to become—people who are more like Christ.

Sometimes we treat our decision to believe in Jesus Christ and the good news of the gospel as if it's a big graduation ceremony, and now we're finished, we've done all we need to do. But maturing in Christ is a lifelong process. When I graduated from seminary, I wore the goofy hat and the goofy gown, and I walked across the stage. However, I knew that I wasn't done as a student. Though I may never go back to a classroom, I would be foolish to think that I was done learning.

Each day, God is looking for areas in our lives that He can continue to shape so that we become more like Jesus. We will never graduate and complete the maturing process in this life. If we submit to the power of the Spirit, it continues until the day we die. God wants us to become people who think like Jesus, talk like Jesus, serve like Jesus, love like Jesus, and have compassion like Jesus.

Real spiritual maturity is a combination of our understanding of theological truth and life transformation based on that truth. Knowledge without life-change is not spiritual maturity. One of the goals of this book is to help us have a greater knowledge of the gospel. However, knowledge of the gospel alone will not lead to spiritual maturity. We must allow not only the truths of the gospel but the entire Bible to shape us to become more faithful disciples of Christ.

I pray that you will examine your life and ask God to give you insight into where He wants you to mature. In my life, God is using Ephesians 4:29, *"Let no corrupting talk come out of your mouths,"* to convict me and point out to me where I need to be growing. This verse is a hard one for me, but as I get rid of the sin of "corrupting talk," I know that God is at work sanctifying me.

God may want you to mature in your knowledge of the scriptures, or He may be asking you to get rid of a certain sin. God may be asking you to give more sacrificially and joyfully, or He may be asking you to spend more time serving your family at home. The gospel, rightfully understood and digested, should impact all these areas of our lives.

Perhaps the maturing process that God wants to take you on today is to help you grow more in love with Jesus and more in love with what He did for you on the cross. In fact, I believe the greatest way we can continue to mature is to make sure that we are bringing ourselves back each day to the death and resurrection of Jesus.

There is no point in trying to grow if our lives aren't going to be centered on the greatness of Christ and His salvation work on the cross. So, never become stagnant in your faith. Instead, fall more in love with the gospel. Each day as you remember what Christ has done for you, respond by surrendering yourself to Him so that He can continue His good work of making you mature in Christ.

Make It Personal

1. Why is it important to God that we never stay stagnant but always keep maturing?

2. Where is God working in your life? In what areas do you need to do some more maturing?

3. How can your love of the gospel impact your willingness to cooperate with God's sanctifying process?

Scriptures to Read

1. John 17

2. Ephesians 4

3. Colossians 1

A Moment of Prayer

- Pray that God will help you to take your spiritual growth seriously.

- Pray that the truths of the gospel will be at the epicenter of your growth.

- Pray that God will empower you to live out your faith in very practical ways.

30

Grace Givers

Matthew 18:21-22

Then Peter came up and said to him, "Lord, how often will my brother sin against me, and I forgive him? As many as seven times?" Jesus said to him, "I do not say to you seven times, but seventy times seven."

After Jesus has this interaction with Peter, in which He exhorts Peter to make forgiveness a lifestyle, He goes on to share what I believe is one of His most powerful parables, "The Parable of the Unforgiving Servant." In this story Jesus speaks of a servant who owed a king 10,000 talents. Since the 10,000 talents couldn't be paid, the king ordered the servant to be sold along with his wife and children in order to cover the debt. On hearing this devastating news, the servant fell to his knees and begged the king to have pity and show patience. He promised that he would somehow find a way to pay back everything he owed. The scripture says, *"And out of pity for him, the master of that servant released him and forgave him the debt"* (Matthew 18:27).

If you have ever owed anyone money, it is always a huge burden until you can figure out a way to pay back what you owe. There's great stress in owing someone money, so being free of a debt is great cause to celebrate and to rejoice, because the burden has been lifted.

The servant in Jesus' parable was forgiven a massive debt. How would you expect Him to respond to his incalculable good fortune? Unfortunately, he didn't respond well. As Jesus continues the parable, He says that the servant went out and *"found one of his fellow servants who owed him a hundred denarii,"* (compared to talents, denarii would be considered pennies) *"and seizing him, he began to choke him, saying, 'Pay what you owe'"* (Matthew 18:28). Though his massive debt had just been forgiven, the servant was unwilling to give that same gift to others.

Jesus wants us to make a connection between this servant and our own lives. We have been given the greatest gift anyone can ask for, complete forgiveness through the debt-paying work of Jesus Christ. Yet there are times when we are stingy in giving others grace.

Paul writes in Colossians,

> *"And you, who were dead in your trespasses and the uncircumcision of your flesh, God made alive together with him, having forgiven us all our trespasses, by canceling the record of debt that stood against us with its legal demands. This he set aside, nailing it to the cross."* (Colossians 2:13–14)

Our sin-deserving debt was nailed to the cross with Christ and wiped off our record. This is the gift that makes the gospel good news.

However, even after benefiting from this massive gift of forgiveness, we still struggle to forgive others, even over the smallest things. People might have hurt us, offended us and even deeply scarred us, but compared to how we have hurt God, compared to what we have been forgiven, it is nothing. There is no comparison between what we have done to God and what others have done to us. Yet, God forgave us and now calls on us, His followers, to offer others the forgiveness He offered to us.

When the gospel truly begins taking root in our lives, one of the fruits will be a willingness to give grace just as God has given grace to us. Our unwillingness to forgive should be seen by us as a clear indication that we haven't fully allowed the gospel to saturate our lives. The more we understand how great our debt to God was, and how great the price Jesus paid to cancel that debt, the more we will see the foolishness of not canceling the debts of others. This doesn't mean we have to be best friends with people who constantly hurt us. This doesn't mean that we stay in relationships that are harmful. But no matter how badly we've been hurt, God's powerful presence in us can give us the capacity to forgive others.

At the end of the parable, the king found out about the servant's sinful behavior and took action. The king said, *"You wicked servant! I forgave you all that debt because you pleaded with me. And should not you have had mercy on your fellow servant, as I had mercy on you?"* (Matthew 18:32–33) The king then had this servant thrown into jail until he could pay back the massive debt he owed, which basically meant that he was never going to be set free. Jesus summarized the king's action by saying, *"So also my heavenly Father will do to every one of you, if you do not forgive your brother from your heart"* (Matthew 18:35).

One of the implications of the gospel taking root in our lives will be seen in our willingness to wipe away the debts of others. Our ability to forgive and give grace is one of the greatest testaments we offer the world about the revolutionary new life we've been given through Christ.

Make It Personal

1. What is the greatest lesson you've learned from the Parable of the Unforgiving Servant?

2. Why should our forgiveness towards others be connected to the forgiveness we have been given by God?

3. Are there people you struggle to forgive? How can focusing on the gospel help you forgive them?

Scriptures to Read

1. Matthew 18

2. Psalm 103

3. John 20

A Moment of Prayer

- Pray that God will help you see that your great debt to God has been canceled through Christ.

- Pray that God would reveal to you people that you have not forgiven.

- Pray that God would empower you to take the steps necessary to forgive them from your heart.

31

Rejoicing in the Gospel

Philippians 1:15–18

Some indeed preach Christ from envy and rivalry, but others from good will. The latter do it out of love, knowing that I am put here for the defense of the gospel. The former proclaim Christ out of rivalry, not sincerely but thinking to afflict me in my imprisonment. What then? Only that in every way, whether in pretense or in truth, Christ is proclaimed, and in that I rejoice.

Does it bring you great joy when the gospel is preached? Oftentimes as Christians, we can be fully engaged in a sermon until the pastor starts teaching on the gospel. That's when we tune out and say, "Oh, I already know this, so I'll check the football scores on my phone." Sometimes pastors neglect the opportunity to preach the good news of Jesus Christ because they are fearful that their church attendees will get bored with hearing the same message over and over. We must get past these dangerously harmful trends and understand that the gospel should be a sweet sound to our ears.

In Paul's letter to the Philippians, he mentions two different types of preachers: those who preach from good will and those who preach out of envy and rivalry. At some level, those who preached from impure motives brought some sort of affliction or pain to Paul while preaching the gospel (they may have spoken poorly of Paul for being in prison). However, no matter what people said or thought of Paul, if the gospel was being proclaimed, it brought Paul joy. I hope to have this same type of gospel focus, so that no matter what is going on in my life, I would rejoice when the gospel is being preached.

The good news of Jesus Christ should never become old news to us. If the gospel doesn't stay fresh in our lives, we will find ourselves in a spiritual desert. We may be looking for some "new and hip" spirituality, but it is the simple and powerful message of the gospel that will bring us great joy and sustain us in all situations.

Paul goes on to say in Philippians 3:8 that he counts "everything as loss because of the surpassing worth of knowing Christ Jesus my Lord." We must remind ourselves each and every day that the gospel is what unites us to God the Father, Jesus Christ His Son, and the Holy Spirit. Without Christ's perfect life, His work on the cross, and resurrection, we would find ourselves alienated from God here on earth and for all eternity.

So, why should we rejoice when we hear the gospel?

1. Because it reminds us of our sin, our need for a Savior, and God's gracious work of sending His Son Jesus Christ to take the punishment we deserve. There is no greater news than that. We should be so grateful every time we're reminded of our salvation through Christ. The truth that we are united with God through Christ should bring us to a joyous worship.

2. Because we know others are listening. When the gospel is preached, there is always a chance that God is in the business of drawing people to Himself. Whenever the gospel is preached, we should be praying that God will allow the good news to fall on fertile soil. It is an awesome experience to be a part of a ministry that leads people to Christ!

3. Because, when the gospel is proclaimed, God gets glory as we lift up His character of love, mercy, grace, justice, holiness, patience, and forgiveness. We should rejoice when we belong to churches that take the gospel seriously, because churches that preach the gospel faithfully get healthier and bring more glory to God.

I pray that we would fall so in love with the gospel that every time we hear it being proclaimed, it will bring us great joy, just as it brought Paul joy while in prison. There should be a sense of excitement, passion, and joyous overflow every time we hear or even read about the truths of the gospel. If you have found yourself lacking joy in the gospel, continue to mediate on its truths, and pray that it will become the central force in your life.

To my non-Christian friends, I pray that God will continue to open your hearts and your minds to the opportunity that you have to be fully reconciled to God through the finished work of Christ.

Make It Personal

1. Why do you think the gospel becomes stale and mundane to us at times?

2. How can you keep the gospel fresh in your spirit at all times?

3. What can you do today to rejoice in the great truths of the gospel?

Scriptures to Read

1. Philippians 1

2. Philippians 3

3. Acts 3

A Moment of Prayer

- Pray that we would be thankful and even rejoice when our churches treat the gospel as the world-changing force it truly is.

- Pray that God would show you when your heart is numb to the gospel.

- Pray that the churches in your community would preach the gospel faithfully and boldly.

32

Satisfied with Christ

Philippians 4:11-13

Not that I am speaking of being in need, for I have learned in whatever situation I am to be content. I know how to be brought low, and I know how to abound. In any and every circumstance, I have learned the secret of facing plenty and hunger, abundance and need. I can do all things through him who strengthens me

My wife and I have a weekly appointment at our favorite Mexican restaurant in South Sacramento. After the chips and salsa, a chicken enchilada, a chile verde quesadilla, beans and rice, and maybe a few more chips to top it off, I am finally satisfied. I am so full that I can barely pay the check and drive home, and when I do get home, the only thing I can think about doing is taking a nap. Though I'm fully content in my overindulgence, my contentment lasts only an hour. Then I need some mint chocolate chip ice cream.

Often, the contentment we experience in this world is as up-and-down as our desires to eat. Though we are satisfied for a moment, there is always something else we suddenly need to make us truly content.

In Philippians 4:11–13, Paul shares the secret of being content in all situations. Whether he had plenty or had nothing, it didn't matter, because he had found contentment in something other than his ever-changing circumstances. The secret of his contentment was Jesus and His salvation.

It is the gospel that brings Paul contentment. This world will always be changing, and our circumstances will always be changing. But no matter our circumstances, you and I can stay content when we understand our undeserved position in Christ.

There are too many times in my life when I'm not experiencing Paul's example of being content in all circumstances. Too often my contentment is based on the relationships around me, my success or failure, or whether or not people see me as being someone important.

I am a pastor to college students, and recently we held one of our college and young adult worship services. Let's just say that, in my eyes, it didn't go as well as I would have liked. Though this happens in ministry, for some reason, I was very discouraged.

It would have been easy to blame the discouragement on a lack of excellence in the programming, or a lack of the kind of passion I wanted to see in the participants, but, being brutally honest with myself, I knew those excuses were not the real source of my discouragement. The real source was my fear of the low opinion people might have of me as the leader because, in my eyes, things didn't go well.

The Lord has been showing me that my identity has become caught up in my ministry, and my contentment goes up and down based on the perceived results. Jesus Christ is confronting me with the gospel truth that He did not come down to Earth and go to the cross to take on my sins, only to have me try to place my sense of worth on my perceived success in my ministry efforts. Jesus' saving grace is what should define me. Jesus' love, suffering, and resurrection should define who I am and how I see myself.

What are the things you think you need to have contentment in your life? We all have a list of things in our head: "If I could just have a new car…," or "If I could just find me a husband…," or "If I could get that new job…then everything would be perfect, and I would be content."

For years, the "thing" in my life was to find a wife. For some of us, the "thing" we feel we need for contentment is finances, or possessions, or relationships, or some form of status. We ignore the gospel and place our identity in this world rather than placing our identity fully in Christ.

I want to get to a place in my life where Jesus is enough and my relationship with God is all that I need to be fully satisfied. I'll always seek to give a great sermon, but I want to get to a place where, whether I'm great or I bomb, I'll be content in Christ. I want to get to the place where, whether hundreds of people come to an event I planned, or just a handful, I'll be content in Christ. I want to get to a place where, whether dinner is good or dinner is forgettable, I'll be content in Christ.

Examine the things in this world that are keeping you from being content and continue to explore the sometimes unfathomable truths of the gospel. Let the gospel's good news become the foundation of your identity and your secret to living with contentment.

Make It Personal

1. Look again at Genesis 3. Why weren't Adam and Eve content with their relationship with God? Do you see where their discontentment took them?

2. What areas of your life are causing discontentment?

3. What can you do to be fully satisfied in Christ and His saving work on the cross?

Scriptures to Read

1. Philippians 4

2. Hebrews 13

3. Genesis 3

A Moment of Prayer

- Pray that you would no longer be controlled by the circumstances of your life.

- Pray that God would reveal to you the sources of your discontentment.

- Pray that God would be your greatest and only source of contentment.

Section Five

Advancing the Gospel

The gospel provides forgiveness of sin, eternal salvation, and reconciliation with God. By God's grace, we have the privilege and the responsibility of partnering with Him to bring this good news and revolutionary message to people who don't know Christ.

Romans 10:13–17

For "everyone who calls on the name of the Lord will be saved." How then will they call on him in whom they have not believed? And how are they to believe in him of whom they have never heard? And how are they to hear without someone preaching? And how are they to preach unless they are sent? As it is written, "How beautiful are the feet of those who preach the good news!" But they have not all obeyed the gospel. For Isaiah says, "Lord, who has believed what he has heard from us?" So faith comes from hearing, and hearing through the word of Christ.

33

Advancing the Gospel

Philippians 1:12–13

I want you to know, brothers, what has happened
to me has really served to advance the gospel,
so that it has become known throughout the
whole imperial guard and to all the rest
that my imprisonment is for Christ.

As Paul wrote his letter to the Philippians, he was most likely sitting in a Roman prison for preaching the gospel. If I were in prison, I'm pretty sure that the last thing I would be thinking would be, "This is a great opportunity to share the gospel with others!" What's more likely is that I would spend my hours and days doing everything I could to prove my innocence and gain my freedom. If it were a movie, there would be this awesome and emotional montage of me studying dusty law books in my dark jail cell and then going out and proving my innocence before the Supreme Court.

Being in jail would overwhelm me, but Paul saw his circumstances as an opportunity to spread the gospel. Paul tells us that because of his imprisonment the gospel had become known throughout the Roman Imperial Guard. Some commentators believe that this means close to 5,000 Roman guards knew of Paul's passion for Christ, and many of them probably heard at least some parts of the gospel.

I wonder how many opportunities God has given us to tell people about the great message of Jesus Christ? Though God may be giving us opportunities, most of us are probably unaware of God's promptings. Worse, many of us are trying to ignore God's call to share the gospel with others.

We sometimes fall into the lie that "regular Christians" don't have to share the gospel; "after all, that's the preacher's job." This type of thinking is the work of Satan and fills our churches with more and more Christians who aren't armed with the powerful message of the gospel. How different would your church look if it were filled with Christians who had the boldness to share Christ at the right opportunities?

The famous 19th-century preacher Charles Spurgeon said that we are all "to be instruments in the hands of God, while (we) actively put forth all the faculties and forces the Lord has lent us. Yet never depend upon your personal power, but rest alone upon the sacred, mysterious, divine energy that works in us, by us, and with us on the hearts and minds of men." Maybe because we depend on our own power rather than the power of God, we end up being weak and timid when it comes to sharing the message that is *the power of God for salvation to everyone who believes* (Romans 1:16).

The revolutionary truth of Jesus Christ should not evoke an attitude of fear that keeps us sitting on our couches all day. When fear keeps me from sharing God's powerful message, I am completely ineffective for the kingdom of God. But once we are gripped by the gospel, we should be moved to bring this good news to others.

Sharing the gospel is often the scariest thing you could ask a Christian to do. However, when the deep realities of the gospel begin to radically transform our lives, we receive a holy burden that reminds us of all the people who need the saving work of Jesus Christ. If we avoid telling people about Christ and His work on the cross, it may be a good indicator that we need to spend more time allowing the gospel to infiltrate our lives. Paul was so consumed by the love of Christ that he lived for opportunities to share the gospel and offer salvation to others. Can we live with that same focus and have a drive to do everything we can to move the gospel forward?

God gave Paul a unique platform for sharing the gospel— a Roman prison. God also gives each of us a unique platform to share the gospel. Your platform may be the people you work with, the students in your classes, your neighbors, or even the people within your church who aren't living fully for Christ. Every opportunity God gives us to build relationships can be an opportunity to advance the gospel. The challenge for us is to open our eyes, allow the Spirit to guide us, and open our mouths to share the great truths of the gospel.

Make It Personal

1. What "platforms" has God given to you to share the gospel?

2. When God gives you the opportunity to share the gospel, do you know what you would say? Spend a few minutes thinking through the clear points that must be communicated in sharing the gospel.

3. What specific fears do you have in sharing the gospel?

Scriptures to Read

1. Philippians 1

2. Romans 1

3. Matthew 28

A Moment of Prayer

- Pray that God would place a burden on you to share the gospel whenever He gives the opportunity.

- Pray that God would give you the boldness to obey Him in sharing the gospel.

- Pray that God would give you great discernment about when and how to share the gospel.

34

Commissioned and Empowered

Acts 1:6-8

So when they had come together, they asked him, "Lord, will you at this time restore the kingdom to Israel?" He said to them, "It is not for you to know times or seasons that the Father has fixed by his own authority. But you will receive power when the Holy Spirit has come upon you, and you will be my witnesses in Jerusalem and in all Judea and Samaria, and to the end of the earth."

The disciples stood in front of Jesus—the same Jesus who days before had been brutally crucified on a cross and placed in a tomb. The doubts that the disciples might have had in Jesus as the long-awaited Messiah were assuredly wiped away as they touched the hands that had been nailed to the cross and touched His side where He had been pierced by a spear. It was within this forty-day post-resurrection ministry that Jesus reminded His disciples of their responsibility to take the good news of the gospel to the world. It would be these disciples, and others committed to following Jesus, who would start the early church and spread the gospel like wildfire.

The disciples were commissioned as witnesses of Jesus. A witness gives an account of a specific event. One may be a witness to a crime or a witness to a car accident. The people of Cleveland used to claim they were all witnesses to the stellar talents of Lebron James. The disciples were witnesses to the teachings and miracles of Jesus, the death of Jesus, and the resurrection of Jesus. Now Jesus tells them to be His *"witnesses in Jerusalem and in all Judea and Samaria, and to the end of the earth."* Because the disciples faithfully carried out this mission in obedience to God, people all over the world have come to know the life-saving power of Jesus Christ and have come to be fully reconciled to God.

If I had been one of these disciples, I would have been terrified by the mission at hand. In one of my first basketball games as a kid, I started crying before the game even started. The coach told me I was going to be one of the five players to start the game and I started crying because I was so nervous. Think about the weight the disciples must have felt on their shoulders when Jesus gave them the assignment of evangelizing the world.

Though Jesus knew He would one day leave His disciples, He also knew that, when He left, He would leave them with the Holy Spirit. Jesus spoke to His disciples and said, *"If you love me, you will keep my commandments. And I will ask the Father, and he will give you another Helper, to be with you forever, even the Spirit of truth, whom the world cannot receive, because it neither sees him nor knows him. You know him, for he dwells with you and will be in you"* (John 14:15–17). When the disciples were given the monumental task of bringing the gospel to the world, they were also given the Holy Spirit to help them accomplish what mere men could never do.

Jesus said (Acts 1:8) that the disciples would receive "power" when the Holy Spirit came upon them. Power was definitely what they would need as they sought to bring Jesus' message to a world that would persecute them for their efforts. Power was what they would need when, at times, they didn't know exactly what to say. Power was what they would need when they didn't know where they should go next or how they should get there. The book of Acts is a testament to the power of the Holy Spirit at work in the disciples as they accomplished the mission of God.

As we go through our days and weeks, months and years, do we sense the power of the Holy Spirit in us to continue what the disciples started? God's mission here on Earth is not finished. There are still people that God wants to call His children. There are still people God is waiting for who need to turn from their sins and trust in Jesus Christ so they can be forgiven and reconciled to God.

If we answer God's call to be His witnesses, we, like the disciples, will undoubtedly feel unqualified and question our ability to be useful for God. However, with the power of the Holy Spirit, you and I can be used by God in ways beyond our imagination.

I'm sure the disciples didn't fully grasp the eternal impact they would have as they shared the truth of the gospel, and I know we will never fully know the impact God will make through us as we share the revolutionary message of Christ crucified. However, let us be less concerned about our impact and more concerned about being obedient to our call of sharing the gospel truth.

I urge you to answer Jesus' marvelous call to be witnesses to the life-changing truths of His gospel. Let us find courage through the Holy Spirit, who has been sent to every believer, not only for our benefit, but for the glory of God and the advancement of His kingdom.

Make It Personal

1. What has Jesus done in your life that you can be a witness to?

2. How do we neglect the power and leadings of the Holy Spirit?

3. What can we do through our church to carry on the work of the disciples?

Scriptures to Read

1. Acts 1

2. John 14

3. Acts 16

A Moment of Prayer

- Pray that God would continue to develop your passion to be His witness.

- Pray that you would be more aware of the supernatural power you have through the Holy Spirit to share the message of the gospel.

- Pray for the people in your life and community who are living outside of the grace of God.

35

Entrusted with the Gospel

1 Thessalonians 2:1–5

*For you yourselves know, brothers, that our coming to you was not
in vain. But though we had already suffered and been shamefully
treated at Philippi, as you know, we had boldness in our God to
declare to you the gospel of God in the midst of much conflict. For
our appeal does not spring from error or impurity or any attempt to
deceive, but just as we have been approved by God to be entrusted
with the gospel, so we speak, not to please man, but to please God
who tests our hearts. For we never came with words of flattery,
as you know, nor with a pretext for greed—God is witness.*

If you have had the privilege of bringing a new life into this
world, you know there is nothing you wouldn't do for the well-
being of that child. Once that child is in your arms for the first
time, there is something that clicks inside you and pushes you to
love and protect as you never have before. You will provide for
your child; you will protect your child; you will nourish your child;
you will cherish your child; and you will do whatever is necessary
to ensure this child has the best life possible. If anything, most
parents probably go a little overboard with all the baby books,
baby monitors, baby laundry detergent, and everything else that
the baby industry has guilt-tripped America into buying.

In Thessalonians 2:1–5, Paul reflects on the purpose and
intentions of his missionary efforts. This passage challenges us
to see that, as followers of Christ, we have been "entrusted" with
the gospel. In the same way that being entrusted with a baby is
an incredible, and sometimes fearful, responsibility, it is also an
incredible, and sometimes fearful, responsibility to be entrusted
with the gospel.

If you are questioning your purpose in life, or questioning whether you could ever do anything of significance, doubt no more. You have been given the mighty role of being entrusted with the gospel. Let's examine several practical ways we can be faithful to this amazing responsibility.

First, show the gospel off. Do everything you can to point people to the good news of Jesus Christ. The gospel is not something we bring out only on Christmas or Easter like those goofy house decorations up in our attics. The gospel is something that should be on display all year long. Look for opportunities to share the gospel, give people books that explain the gospel, and invite people to churches that preach the gospel.

Show off the gospel as the most valuable possession in your life. Instead of showing off things that we have accumulated or accomplished in this world, we should be showing off what Christ has accomplished on our behalf. We can be people God uses to humbly boast in the divinity of Christ, the holiness of Christ, the sacrifice of Christ, and the resurrection of Christ. Most of us aren't theologians or preachers, but none of us can go wrong with simply sharing these truths with the people God has placed in our lives. Our desire to show off the gospel is an act of worship, and God will use our efforts and passion to bring people closer to Himself.

Second, protect the gospel. Don't allow the gospel to become something it isn't. We protect the gospel by making sure nothing is added to or subtracted from the great truths we find in scripture. Paul writes, *"but just as we have been approved by God to be entrusted with the gospel, so we speak, not to please man, but to please God who tests our hearts"* (1 Thessalonians 2:4).

Often, in our fear of talking about sin, repentance, and Jesus' death on the cross, we morph the gospel into something that is palatable for others to swallow and digest. We mustn't worry about whether or not people will accept the truths of the gospel. It is God's role to open their eyes and hearts, and it is their responsibility to faithfully respond.

Our responsibility is to be faithful in presenting the whole truth of the gospel. The more we worry about offending people or worry about what they might think of us, the further we move away from sharing the great truths of what Christ did to bring us everlasting life and reconciliation with God.

Third, cherish the gospel. The gospel has to become our greatest joy. It should be the sweetest sound to our ears and the greatest taste to our mouths. The more we immerse ourselves in understanding the gospel, the more it is going to completely revolutionize our lives. To cherish the gospel is to fall more in love with God and the sacrifice He has made for us. When we cherish the gospel, we will be blessed with peace and joy in our own lives, and we will seek to propel the gospel forward to bless the world.

We have been entrusted with the gospel. What an amazing gift and responsibility! I pray that you will take your responsibility seriously by showing the gospel off, protecting the gospel, and cherishing the gospel.

Make It Personal

1. What would you do if someone entrusted you with their child before they passed away? How does that compare to God entrusting you with the gospel? Do you feel the weight and significance of that responsibility?

2. What is one way you can show the gospel off this week?

3. What happens if the gospel gets morphed into something that doesn't align with scripture?

Scriptures to Read

1. 1 Thessalonians 2

2. Galatians 2

3. 2 Corinthians 2

A Moment of Prayer

- Pray that God would continue to show you what an honor and responsibility it is to be entrusted with the gospel.

- Pray that you would protect the gospel at all cost.

- Pray that God would continue to awaken your passion and love for the gospel.

36

The Power Is in the Message

1 Corinthians 2:1–5

And I, when I came to you, brothers, did not come proclaiming to you the testimony of God with lofty speech or wisdom. For I decided to know nothing among you except Jesus Christ and him crucified. And I was with you in weakness and in fear and much trembling, and my speech and my message were not in plausible words of wisdom, but in demonstration of the Spirit and of power, that your faith might not rest in the wisdom of men but in the power of God.

As we reflect on this scripture, it is humbling that Paul, one of the great heroes of the New Testament, writes about the weaknesses and fears he feels when communicating the gospel. Many of us can relate to feeling fearful and inadequate when sharing the gospel. However, we are called by God, despite our hesitations, to be His witnesses to those who are facing eternal death.

As we face our calling, I think we can learn from Paul. He knew that he was weak, but he learned how to trust in the strength of God when sharing the gospel. I want to make a couple of observations from this passage in 1 Corinthians.

First, Paul was committed to a simple but powerful message: "Jesus Christ and him crucified." That message is at the core of the gospel. There is nothing more important to the message we share than what Christ did on the cross to pay for our sins and reconcile us to God. Today, there are so many different messages that we can find ourselves communicating something very different than the message that God wants us to be most concerned with—the gospel. We can get too caught up in social justice issues, politics, or the latest self-help fad while letting the simple but revolutionary message of the gospel get pushed aside. To be effective, biblical, and God-honoring, we must be resolute in not abandoning the only message that has the power to save its listeners. Paul writes, *"For I am not ashamed of the gospel, for it is the power of God for salvation to everyone who believes"* (Romans 1:16). Are you living ashamed of the powerful message of the gospel?

My second observation is that God uses us in our weaknesses. Obviously Paul wasn't a perfect communicator, yet God chose to use Him in his imperfections. Often, when we think about sharing the gospel, our attention and focus becomes so much about us. We worry and stress about our gifts and our abilities instead of being focused on the Spirit who uses us in our weakness. Instead of being humbled by the opportunity to share the gospel, we become self-focused and concerned about what we think we can or cannot do. Rather than being people who place their confidence in God's power, we become paralyzed by our fears or run away from opportunities to advance the gospel because we lack confidence in our abilities.

We need to remember that we have been saved by God's grace, not our greatness, and that we live by God's grace, not our strengths. In His grace, God chose to use us to share the good news; it was not because of our amazing gifts and abilities. So, let's get over ourselves, stop worrying about our weaknesses, and trust God's grace to work through us as we share the good news.

My third observation is that God's power should be reflected in our efforts to share the gospel. Remember, it is not about our abilities; it is all about God and His ability to work through sinners like us.

Paul says it this way to the Corinthians who were starting to divide over whose style of sharing the gospel was the best: *"I planted, Apollos watered, but God gave the growth. So neither he who plants nor he who waters is anything, but only God who gives the growth"* (1 Corinthians 3:6–7). Paul wants to make it clear: it is God who does the work, and it is God who deserves the glory. This means that when we see the fruit of our efforts at sharing the good news, or the fruit of someone else's efforts, we should be quick to praise God and not get prideful in "our success" or jealous of someone else's. Remember, the power is in the message, not in the messenger.

I know that when I start thinking that I have to depend on my gifts and talents to be effective in sharing the gospel, I can be crippled by fear and talk myself out of being faithful to my responsibilities. In other instances, I take the credit and praise for my "success" in sharing the gospel, praise that only God deserves. Let us commit ourselves to never wavering from the central truth of the gospel, and let us rely on the strength of God, not our own strength, to share this powerful truth with others.

Make It Personal

1. Why do you think Paul was fearful at times in sharing the gospel?

2. Why is staying on message so important?

3. What can you do to depend more on God's abilities rather than your own when sharing the gospel?

Scriptures to Read

1. 1 Corinthians 2

2. 1 Corinthians 3

3. Galatians 6

A Moment of Prayer

- Pray that God will help you stay focused on the central truths of the gospel.

- Pray that you would see God's desire to work through you as you tell others about Jesus.

- Pray that you would never be crippled by your fear of sharing the gospel.

Boasting in the Cross

Galatians 6:13–16

For even those who are circumcised do not themselves keep the law, but they desire to have you circumcised that they may boast in your flesh. But far be it from me to boast except in the cross of our Lord Jesus Christ, by which the world has been crucified to me, and I to the world. For neither circumcision counts for anything, nor uncircumcision, but a new creation. And as for all who walk by this rule, peace and mercy be upon them, and upon the Israel of God.

In our world of entertainment, it seems like you can't become someone famous unless you're willing to make Muhammad Ali–type claims about your greatness. Pride lies at the center of each of our hearts, and whether or not we claim to be the greatest, we all find ourselves boasting about something. I used to claim to be the greatest basketball player; then I reached the fourth grade and discovered, to my dismay, that there were bigger and faster players on the playground.

Before Paul had his miraculous and life-changing encounter with Jesus Christ on the road to Damascus (Acts 9), he was a Jew who was proud of his family background, superior education, rising reputation, and religious zeal. Paul's zeal unfortunately led to the persecution of Christians (Philippians 3:1–8). However, Paul's encounter with Christ transformed Him. Paul realized that what once seemed valuable to him was absolutely worthless in comparison to what he had received from Christ. After encountering the reality of the gospel, Paul's values were redefined and he boasted only in Christ and the cross.

We, like the old Paul, often find ourselves boasting in our latest accomplishments, our newest purchases, and the friends we hope will make us seem more important than we really are. However, can you imagine standing at the foot of the cross and witnessing the most staggering event in all of human history? When we sit at the scene of the cross by mediating on what scripture teaches us, it makes all the things we formerly thought were important seem utterly insignificant.

We must ask the Holy Spirit to help us never wander away from this glorious focal point in history. Satan would love for us to get distracted and lose focus on what is actually important, but we must fix our eyes on Christ and what He accomplished through His death and resurrection. It is at the scene of the cross where we realize that it is hard for us to boast in anything but what Christ has done for us. Theologian and pastor Martyn Lloyd Jones, referring to the cross, says that, "The test of the Christian is that he glories in it (the cross), he exults it, he boasts of it. It is everything to him, without it he has nothing. He owes all to this, this cross is the center of his universe in every respect." To boast in the cross means that Christ's work on the cross has become such a focal point in your life that you can't help but proclaim the truths of gospel through the way you live and the things you say.

Often, we define our value through things like our careers, our finances, our families—whatever is most valuable to us. Because we derive our sense of value from these things, they are the things that we become prideful of and boast about. I admit that I am not immune to boasting about things that make me feel like I'm somebody important. I struggle in this area of my life, and I find myself at times boasting in my ministry or educational successes. I am convinced that I need to boast less in my latest accomplishments and boast more in what Christ has done for me and others. Hopefully, by God's grace I can start to live with Paul's simple but powerful focus, *"For I decided to know nothing among you except Jesus Christ and him crucified"* (1 Corinthians 2:2).

When we stand before the God of the universe one day, we

will have a choice: we can boast in what we've done, or we can boast in what His Son has done for us. That choice is completely ours. We can choose to let our eternal destiny stand on our accomplishments, or to let our eternal destiny stand on the great work of Jesus Christ. What are you planning to boast about?

When we allow the great news of the gospel to become the center of our identity and purpose here on Earth, we will begin to boast in the life-changing power of the cross at every opportunity. So, let us become boastful, but not in ourselves. Instead, choose to boast in the cross of Jesus Christ; it is the only thing worth boasting in.

Make It Personal

1. Do you spend more time boasting in your accomplishments or Christ's accomplishments?

2. Why are we sometimes ashamed to boast in the cross?

3. How will focusing on the gospel's message help you to boast less about yourself and more about Jesus? What will you do to make this happen?

Scriptures to Read

1. Acts 9

2. Galatians 3

3. Galatians 6

A Moment of Prayer

- Pray that God would humble you so that you will boast less about yourself and more about the cross.

- Pray that you will learn to value things from the viewpoint of what Christ has done for you.

- Pray that you would never abandon the gospel for something you thought was more important.

38

Preach the Word

Romans 10:13-17

For "everyone who calls on the name of the Lord will be saved."
How then will they call on him in whom they have not believed?
And how are they to believe in him of whom they have never
heard? And how are they to hear without someone preaching?
And how are they to preach unless they are sent? As it is written,
"How beautiful are the feet of those who preach the good news!"
But they have not all obeyed the gospel. For Isaiah says, "Lord,
who has believed what he has heard from us?" So faith comes
from hearing, and hearing through the word of Christ.

We cannot run away from our call to be preachers of the Word. When I suggest that we are all called to preach the Word, I'm not suggesting that we all need to become pastors or that we all need to preach the next sermon at our local church. The call to be a pastor isn't for everyone and the call to preach isn't everyone's gift. However, all followers of Christ are called to proclaim the truth of the gospel with passion and precision.

For the last two years, my wife and I have brought groups to New Orleans on a week-long mission trip. New Orleans is still plagued by the impact of Hurricane Katrina, and the Hollygrove neighborhood, where we have ministered, is also plagued by drugs, alcohol, violence, and poverty. In the middle of that neighborhood is a little organization called Trinity Christian Community (TCC). TCC has, for decades, been a glimmer of hope in this seemingly decaying neighborhood as it seeks to meet the demanding physical needs of the community. But while they deal with physical needs, they never shy away from their commitment to bring the gospel to their community.

Partnering with this organization has given our teams a perfect balance between serving the physical needs of the community in the aftermath of Katrina and providing countless opportunities to meet the spiritual and eternal needs of the community. In our pre-trip training, we spent months reminding our teams that there were countless groups going to New Orleans to assist after the hurricane, but our group had the additional call to bring the good news of the gospel. It was the gospel that had the power to truly transform the neighborhood.

Maybe it's because of our countless fears about sharing the gospel that there seems to have been a movement to replace evangelism with good works. Instead of fulfilling our call to advance the kingdom through the proclamation of the whole gospel, we, at times, believe that meeting someone's physical needs or fighting for social justice is enough.

When we look at Romans 10:13–17, we see an undeniable connection between comprehending the truths of the gospel and making a conscious decision to turn and follow Jesus. How will people hear of their sin if all we do is give them food? How will they know of their need for a Savior if all we do is give them clean water? How will they know who Jesus is, and why Jesus came, if all we do is rebuild their house?

Good works and social justice are necessary. They are the results that come when the gospel takes the central role in our lives. But we must be clear and not call these types of efforts evangelism or the proclamation of the gospel.

We probably all lack confidence in the area of sharing the gospel. We must take the steps necessary to hurdle any roadblocks that keep us from being faithful to our call to evangelize. What efforts are you making to grow in your passion to share the gospel? What are you doing to increase the clarity and effectiveness of your sharing?

We spend countless hours trying to stay in shape, excel in higher education, or advance in the workplace. Why wouldn't we have that same passion for developing our ability to communicate the greatest truths this world will ever hear? Do you really want to stand before God one day feeling that you didn't put in your best effort at answering God's call to share the good news with the people He has strategically brought into your life?

I pray that God will continue to work in your life so that you will not treat the gospel as if it were something to be kept in a jar for yourself, but will instead feel compelled to proclaim the gospel to everyone. Jesus said, *"You are the light of the world. A city set on a hill cannot be hidden. Nor do people light a lamp and put it under a basket, but on a stand, and it gives light to all in the house"* (Matthew 5:14–15). If we are going to proclaim the gospel, we need to know the gospel, love the gospel, and truly believe that its message alone can provide salvation and reconcile people to a thriving relationship with God.

Make It Personal

1. Why can't social action and good works replace evangelism and preaching?

2. Do you believe that sharing and preaching the gospel are important?

3. What practical steps can you take to build your confidence in sharing the gospel?

Scriptures to Read

1. Romans 10

2. 2 Timothy 4

3. Titus 1

A Moment of Prayer

- Pray that you would understand your role as a preacher of God's Word.

- Pray that you would come to love and be passionate about all of God's Word.

- Pray that you would see that the gospel should be the central focus of your preaching.

39

Serving Others

James 2:14-17

*What good is it, my brothers, if someone says he has faith but
does not have works? Can that faith save him? If a brother
or sister is poorly clothed and lacking in daily food, and one of
you says to them, "Go in peace, be warmed and filled," without
giving them the things needed for the body, what good is that?
So also faith by itself, if it does not have works, is dead.*

Though we have spent a considerable amount of time looking
at the truths of the gospel and our call to advance the gospel, we
must also see our need to serve others for the sake of the gospel.
Serving others is not sharing the gospel, but God can use our
service to prepare people to hear the gospel. We must be certain,
however, to put the emphasis in the right place. If the emphasis
is on the serving, we could begin to view our good works as our
hope for salvation. Another danger of having a wrong emphasis
is that we could view our good works as a replacement for sharing the gospel. However, when we appropriately emphasize good
works as something we do in support of the proclamation of the
gospel, we live out a more holistic approach to our Christian
faith.

James reminds Christians that faith without good works is
really no faith at all. He writes, *"So also faith by itself, if it does not
have works, is dead"* (James 2:17). Follow me on this: A love for
the gospel, without a commitment to serve others, means that
you really don't love the gospel. The greatest way Christ served us
was by going to the cross. However, during His three-year ministry He also looked to serve people in very simple and practical
ways.

If we use Christ as our example, we will recognize that the greatest way we can serve others is by bringing them the good news of the gospel. However, just as Christ did, we will also look to serve others in practical ways as well. If we truly have embraced and been transformed by the truths of the gospel, we will look to serve others without expecting anything in return.

My brother Greg is a great example to me of someone who has figured out how to serve people while never backing away from sharing the gospel. People of all types gravitate to Greg because he genuinely cares deeply about them. Greg listens to them and always figures out a way to serve them, whether that means buying them a meal, giving them a book, or giving them a ride to work.

Because Greg takes the time to build relationships with people, when the Spirit leads him, he is able to share with them about his love and passion for Jesus and Jesus' love and passion for the world. Greg's example inspires me to live out my faith in more practical ways by looking for opportunities to serve people, and challenges me to share my faith with zeal and conviction.

Our good works can often lead people to have a more receptive response to the gospel message when we share it with them. God will use our genuine concern for people to prepare their hearts and minds to hear the gospel. People need the gospel more than anything this world can offer, yet at times we may be overlooking God's call to serve people in their needs.

Jesus has taught us, *"In the same way, let your light shine before others, so that they may see your good works and give glory to your Father who is in heaven"* (Matthew 5:16). Serving people should be an expression of our love for Jesus Christ, and I believe we will be surprised at the ways God will use our good works to open doors to share the greatest news this world could ever hear, the good news of the gospel.

Make It Personal

1. How can our good works help others become receptive to hearing the gospel message?

2. How can good works be an indication that the gospel is making a difference in your life?

3. How can you serve the people in your circles of influence?

Scriptures to Read

1. Matthew 5

2. Matthew 25

3. 1 Peter 2

A Moment of Prayer

- Pray that you would never overlook an opportunity to serve people, but that you would also never replace your evangelism with service.

- Pray that God would reveal to you practical ways you can serve and care for others.

- Praise God for the people who have served you and shared the gospel with you so that you could have a saving faith in Him.

40

For His Praise

Psalm 29:1-2

Ascribe to the LORD, O heavenly beings,
ascribe to the LORD glory and strength.
Ascribe to the LORD the glory due his name;
worship the LORD in the splendor of holiness.

Throughout scripture, God shows His desire to be worshiped. God always wants to be the focus of our worship because He is the mighty, holy Creator, Savior, and Lord of the universe and beyond. A failure to worship God is a failure to understand who God is. Worship is also what should motivate us to advance and share the good news of the gospel.

Sometimes, when we are sharing the gospel with others, it can easily become focused on our efforts. We are concerned about how well we share the gospel. We are concerned about how many people have committed their lives to Christ after we have shared the gospel with them compared to how many people others have led to Christ. We then become prideful about how many people have come to know the Lord because of our evangelistic endeavors. Psalm 29 speaks of giving God the glory that is *"due His name."* When our focus is on ourselves, we are failing to give God the worship that is rightly His—we are stealing His glory.

Sometimes our motivations to share the good news are driven by the blessings people will experience if they repent and place their faith in Christ. We strongly desire for our friends and loved ones to experience forgiveness, eternal salvation, and the joy of walking with God. These are incredible blessings that we should want others to experience. These blessings should motivate us to share the gospel. But let me suggest to you that our greatest motivation should be to see people turn from worshiping themselves and the things of the world to worshiping the true and living God. We should have such a deep awareness of God's worthiness to be worshiped that we are troubled when our holy God isn't getting the glory that He deserves. Do you want God to receive worship from the people in your life who are currently turning their backs on Him?

If our efforts to advance the gospel aren't marked by a desire to bring more people into the worship of God, we can compromise the message. We can be so concerned about getting people to "cross the line," that we get tempted to soften the call of following Jesus at all cost. Instead, we list off all the blessings salvation brings and ask people to pray a "prayer of salvation" but fail to tell them that they have to leave everything to follow Christ and that they have to turn from sin and live their lives in complete worship of God. Our message should include the amazing blessings of the gospel—that's why it is called good news—but we must make sure that our message is rightly accompanied with the call to worship God, which is also good news and a blessing.

The picture of Christ in Philippians 2 gives us insight into why and how we worship God:

> *And being found in human form, he humbled himself by becoming obedient to the point of death, even death on a cross. Therefore God has highly exalted him and bestowed on him the name that is above every name, so that at the name of Jesus every knee should bow, in heaven and on earth and under the earth, and every tongue confess that Jesus Christ is Lord, to the glory of God the Father.* (Philippians 2:8–11)

I pray that our lives will be marked by an extreme desire to worship the God of our salvation. I also pray that we will understand that the call to bring the good news of the gospel to the world is not about us; it is a call to bring more people to the throne of God in complete worship of Him.

Make It Personal

1. Do you believe that God deserves worship from all people? Why?

2. How does it make you feel when people don't worship God?

3. What can you do today to worship God more fully and help others worship God more fully?

Scriptures to Read

1. Psalm 29

2. Romans 12

3. Revelation 21

A Moment of Prayer

- Pray that God will bring you to a deeper worship of Him as the gospel revolutionizes your life.

- Pray that you would have a great burden for people everywhere to give God the worship that is due His name.

- Pray that God would reveal to you how all aspects of your life can be turned into worship of Him.

Conclusion

Never Grow Tired of the Gospel

# Never Grow Tired of the Gospel

I wrote this book with the hope that a few more people would come to a place of living in absolute amazement of what Christ has done for us, and that we would marvel at how our lives can be completely changed by the life, death, and resurrection of Jesus. I have seen this transformation happen in my life and in the lives of others.

Through the work of the Holy Spirit, God has opened our eyes to the reality that we are deeply wicked sinners in need of a Savior. We need a Savior because our Holy God must punish our sins. But God, in His love, sent His perfect Son, to live the life we should have lived and die the death we should have died. As we became more aware of who we were and what we deserved, the grace of God, seen through the gospel, became the sweetest truth we've ever known and it has changed our lives forever.

I pray that the Holy Spirit has worked in your life as you read through this book by making you more aware of how wicked you can be, but how great, holy, perfect and loving God is. I pray that the gospel not only leads you to repentance, faith and salvation, but that the gospel continues to transform you into the worshiper God wants you to be. Finally, I pray that you will never grow tired of the revolutionary message of the gospel, but will keep it fresh and alive in your heart every day.

In conclusion, I want to give you a few different exercises that will help you to reflect on, remember, and rejoice in the glorious truths of Christ crucified.

These are exercises that I have learned over the last couple of years from reading great books on the gospel and listening to great gospel preaching. I pray that you will use all of these exercises to keep the good news of your salvation, through Jesus' life, death, and resurrection, on the forefront of your heart, mind, and soul.

1. Pray the Gospel

I can't think of anything more valuable at the start of each day than praying through the truths of the gospel. Often in the busyness of life we wake up and our minds and bodies start working towards accomplishing the tasks of the day. We are so quick to start crossing off things on our "to-do lists" that we forget about the most important aspect of our lives: that we have been saved from God's wrath by God's grace, through the work of Jesus Christ on the cross.

How would your day be different if you always started it by praising God for His love, mercy, and grace? We need perspective in the midst of our crazy lives. If you pray the gospel, I believe God will help you have the perspective, worldview, and mindset you will need to live for Him and bring Him glory. So start your day by thanking and praising God for what He has specifically done to reconcile your relationship to Himself and to give you eternal life through Jesus Christ alone.

Below is an example of a prayer that can help you keep the gospel at the center of your life each and every day. This is not a prayer for you to memorize but an example of a prayer that you can use.

"God, I thank you and praise you for the new life I have in you. Before I placed my faith in your Son Jesus Christ, I was an absolute sinner who loved to live completely disobedient to your ways. Even now I struggle with sin, yet through your grace and mercy my eyes have been opened to my need for a Savior. Thank you for sending your only Son down to earth to live a perfect life and die a sinner's death.

"Though I am forever grateful for His death on the cross, I know I deserve the wrath that He received from you. I am grateful for the obedience of Christ to willingly submit himself to the cross so that my sins could be punished. I am grateful for the perfectly obedient life of Christ that allows His righteousness to be counted as my righteousness. Lord, I am grateful for the gospel and all the implications that come with being saved by you and adopted into your family.

"Give me strength and guidance from your Holy Spirit so that today I can honor you above all else in light of what you have done for me. Today, if I have opportunities, give me the courage to tell others about the good news of your Son Jesus Christ.

"As I go throughout my day, let me continually rejoice in the truth that I have a real relationship with you because of your grace and because of Christ's work on the cross. Amen."

2. Memorize Gospel Verses

There are great benefits to memorizing specific scriptures that bring to light the truths of the gospel. The verses below are a good place to start, but obviously not an exhaustive list. Allow your heart and mind to soak in the glorious truths found in God's Word; this will help you to remember who you are and what God has done for you. Through the transforming work of the Spirit and your effort to memorize scriptures that focus on the gospel, you will see God awaken your soul to what Christ has done to give you forgiveness of sins and reconciliation with God. Memorizing these verses will also give you greater readiness and confidence in sharing the gospel with others.

Tools and resources to aid in scripture memorization are numerous. Two to consider are the Navigators Topical Memory System (available at www.cbd.com) and the free online memorization site: www.memverse. com

Mark 10:45 *"For even the Son of Man came not to be served but to serve, and to give his life as a ransom for many."*

Romans 3:23–25a *For all have sinned and fall short of the glory of God, and are justified by his grace as a gift, through the redemption that is in Christ Jesus, whom God put forward as a propitiation by his blood, to be received by faith.*

1 Timothy 2:3–6 *This is good, and it is pleasing in the sight of God our Savior, who desires all people to be saved and to come to the knowledge of the truth. For there is one God, and there is one mediator between God and men, the man Christ Jesus, who gave himself as a ransom for all, which is the testimony given at the proper time.*

1 Corinthians 15:3–4 *For I delivered to you as of first importance what I also received: that Christ died for our sins in accordance with the Scriptures, that he was buried, that he was raised on the third day in accordance with the Scriptures.*

Acts 3:19–20 *Repent therefore, and turn again, that your sins may be blotted out, that times of refreshing may come from the presence of the Lord, and that he may send the Christ appointed for you, Jesus.*

Ephesians 2:4–5 *But God, being rich in mercy, because of the great love with which he loved us, even when we were dead in our trespasses, made us alive together with Christ—by grace you have been saved.*

Hebrews 4:15 *For we do not have a high priest who is unable to sympathize with our weaknesses, but one who in every respect has been tempted as we are, yet without sin.*

Isaiah 53:5–6 *But he was wounded for our transgressions; he was crushed for our iniquities; upon him was the chastisement that brought us peace, with his stripes we are healed. All we like sheep have gone astray; we have turned—every one—to his own way; and the LORD has laid on him the iniquity of us all.*

1 John 1:7–9 *But if we walk in the light, as he is in the light, we have fellowship with one another, and the blood of Jesus his Son cleanses us from all sin. If we say we have no sin, we deceive ourselves, and the truth is not in us. If we confess our sins, he is faithful and just to forgive us our sins and to cleanse us from all unrighteousness.*

Revelation 1:5b–6 *To him who loves us and has freed us from our sins by his blood and made us a kingdom, priests to his God and Father, to him be glory and dominion forever and ever.*

3. Preach the Gospel to Yourself

Preaching the gospel to ourselves is a simple but practical discipline that I have learned from the writings of Jerry Bridges and C. J. Mahaney. Instead of being people who wait for the Sunday sermon to remind us of the core truths of the gospel, we should be people who remind ourselves of these truths each and every day. I need to remind myself of my sin, God's grace, and Christ's work on the cross. Every once in a while my neighbors probably hear me preaching to myself as I walk back and forth in our backyard. Sunday church services cannot be our only fueling of these truths. If we only hear these truths occasionally, we will slowly drift away from the cross and the resurrection.

On a practical level, we can often find ourselves feeling shamed and condemned for the sins in our lives. It is at these moments that we need to preach to ourselves about the grace, forgiveness, and freedom that are found in the cross.

There are days when we feel lonely and unloved. It is at these times that we need to remind ourselves that God loved us so much that He was willing to send His one and only Son to the cross so that we can be reconciled into a deep relationship with Him.

There are times when we are struggling to understand our purpose in life. It is at these times that we need to preach the gospel to ourselves and be reminded that our entire lives should be focused on bringing glory to God and to advancing the gospel here on Earth.

Few of us would consider ourselves preachers, but there is nothing keeping us from challenging ourselves to remember and live in light of what Christ has done for us.

4. Rejoice in Gospel Preaching

There are times in our immaturity when we want to hear something new and exciting preached on Sunday. So, upon hearing the gospel, we quickly close our hearts because it is something that we already know and think we have mastered. When the gospel is being preached, we say to ourselves, "Oh, this is the part of the sermon for the non-believers and I don't have to pay attention," and we start doodling in our sermon notes.

In maturity, let us be people who pay more attention when we hear our pastors expounding on the gospel. We need to be reminded of the truths we already know, and we need to learn the more intricate details that we often overlook. If we find ourselves struggling to learn and grow during a sermon that points us to the cross, we should pray to God and ask Him to open our minds and hearts to receive the truth that is being preached.

I would also challenge you to encourage your pastors as they seek to help the congregation fall more in love with the gospel. You can encourage them by paying close attention, taking notes, and thanking them for always reminding you of the most important aspect of living out your Christian faith. Pray that your pastors and leaders will preach the fullness of the gospel with great courage and that your congregation would come to fall in love with such teaching.

5. Give to the Advancement of the Gospel

The final discipline that I would encourage you to bring into your daily and weekly routine is the act of being involved in gospel advancement. We can't hoard the gospel and keep it to ourselves. We should be on an absolute mission to see the gospel spread to those who are currently perishing without the good news of Jesus Christ.

To get involved in the advancement of the gospel, we must seek the wisdom of God and our church leaders to determine how God would like to use us each day of our lives. We must ask the question, "God, how do you want to use me today to bring light to this world so that more and more people will come to know you through repentance and faith in Christ?"

Here is a list of things that God may be asking you to do throughout your day or week:

- Share the gospel with someone.
- Give financially to your church and to other organizations that are preaching and advancing the gospel.
- Provide an unbeliever with a book, sermon, or Bible that will help them understand the gospel.
- Pray for those in your life who don't know Christ, and ask God to open their eyes to the gospel.
- Use your gifts and talents at your local church. By using your talents within the local church, you will strengthen your church's effectiveness in reaching more people.
- Disciple a young believer to understand and grow more passionate about the fullness of the gospel.

These are just a few examples of how you can be involved in the advancement of the gospel. We know from scripture that

God's desire is for more and more people to be saved and that He uses us as His ambassadors of the gospel. Some of the examples above are more difficult than others, but we seek courage from our God so that we will be bold in our faith and follow in Paul's example: "For I am not ashamed of the gospel, for it is the power of God for salvation to everyone who believes" (Romans 1:16).

A Final Prayer

God, raise up for yourself more and more people who are passionate about the gospel of Jesus Christ. Help us to become a people who don't move on from the gospel but constantly live in awe of what we have been given through your plan to save sinners through Christ Jesus. Lord, we want to understand the gospel more fully so that we can communicate it more faithfully. We want the gospel to be so ingrained into our hearts and minds that it is at the center of everything we do. We want the gospel of grace to be the source of our worship, good works, and obedience to you. Never let us do anything to try to earn your blessings or your approval, but let us do everything in light of what you have done for us. Let the gospel revolutionize every aspect of our lives: our thinking, our living, our relationships, our finances, our careers, our commitment to you, our worship, our marriages, our families, our obedience, our joy, our peace, our purpose, and what should be our greatest treasure—You. Let the gospel completely and utterly change us until the day in which we are fully reconciled to You for eternity.

Father, we praise you and rejoice in what you have done for us. Without you we are lost. Without you we are dead. However, with you, and because of you and your Son Jesus Christ, we have everything.

Jesus, we thank you for your perfect life and for your willingness to go to the cross to receive the wrath of God that should be poured out on us. We praise you for your complete obedience. We are humbled by your love for us. We rejoice in the salvation we have only because of your substitutionary work on the cross.

Holy Spirit, guide us and lead us to live in response to the gospel. Sanctify us to become more holy and more righteous. Empower us to live more boldly for the advancement of the good news of Jesus Christ. And help us to always rejoice and never move on from the glorious truth of the gospel. Amen.

Making the Greatest Decision Ever

The Decision to Fully Trust
in the Work of Christ

If you have never turned from your sin and placed your faith in Christ, there is no better time than now to make the greatest decision ever. There is nothing magical about becoming a Christian; all you have to do is:

1. Repent of Your Sin

Recognize that you are a sinner—someone that has disobeyed and ignored God and His standards. Renounce your old ways of living and commit yourself to living a life that is honoring to God.

2. Place Your Faith in Christ

Place your faith in the sinless life of Christ, His death on the cross as your deserved punishment, and His resurrection from the dead. As you place your faith in Christ, you are trusting that there is nothing you can do to earn God's favor. It is only through the work of Christ that you will be declared righteous and forgiven. Placing your faith in Christ means you understand that it is only through the work of Christ that you are reconciled to God and promised eternal life.

Are you ready to make this decision? It's simple, yet monumental. You do it by talking to God, telling Him that you are repenting of your sin, putting your faith in Christ, and committing yourself to following Jesus wholeheartedly. Below is a prayer you can use as a guideline for putting your faith in Christ and committing yourself to following Him.

A Salvation Prayer

God, today I recognize that I have ignored You and sinned against You. I repent of my sin. I renounce my sin. Give me the strength to turn from my sin and to live a life that is fully honoring to You.

Today, I place my faith not in myself, but in the life, death, and resurrection of Jesus Christ. I understand that it was upon the cross that my sin was punished by Your wrath, and I rejoice in my Savior Jesus, who was willing to be my sacrifice. I know I don't deserve it, but I am forever grateful for what Christ has done to bring me to You.

I praise You and love You. Amen.

If you have made this decision today, praise God! There is no greater decision you can ever make. Welcome to the family of God.

Now, I have a couple of challenges for you.

1. Make sure you let a committed follower of Christ know that you have made this decision, and ask them what steps you should take next.
2. Join a local, gospel-believing church. It is critical for your growth and for the growth of God's kingdom that you become an active and committed member of a local church.

GOSPEL
REVOLUTION
ALLOWING GOD TO AWAKEN OUR PASSION FOR THE GOSPEL

STUDY GUIDE

Study #1

God of the Gospel

1. What role does the gospel play in your life? Is the gospel something that you are passionate about? Why is the gospel something that we often forget or neglect to meditate on?

2. Why is understanding the character of God important to fully understanding the gospel? How would we miss out on some of the nuances of the gospel if we didn't know the God of the gospel?

Read Genesis 1:26–27.

3. We as humans are at the pinnacle of God's creation. We are made in the image of God and created to be in a deep relationship with God. Do you see God as someone wanting to be in a relationship with you?

Read Deuteronomy 4:23–24.

4. What are the "carved images" in your life?

5. What does it mean that God is a jealous God? Why would God be jealous when we choose other things or people over Him?

6. How can you re-prioritize your relationship with God?

Read Acts 17:30-31.

7. How would our lives change if we never forgot that one of God's roles is that of judge? What criteria will God use to judge us?

8. How can we have the "assurance" that is spoken of in this passage?

Read 1 John 4:8-11.

9. How does the gospel highlight God's love for us?

10. Why would it serve us well to reflect on God's love seen through what Christ did for us on the cross?

MAKE IT PRACTICAL

11. Come up with a list of things that often become more important to you than your relationship with God? Pray over this list. Repent and ask God for the wisdom, desire, and strength to always keep Him as your highest treasure, greatest joy, and top priority.

Study #2

The Grand Dilemma

1. The Grand Dilemma is that we have all sinned and God must punish sin. Why is it important to have a strong understanding of sin and how it impacts our relationship with God? How would you define sin?

2. What happens if we have a shallow or unrealistic view of our sin?

Read Romans 3:9–26.

3. What does it mean that all "are under sin" (v. 9)?

4. What type of picture does Paul paint of humanity in verses 10–18?

5. How are we going to "be held accountable to God" (v. 19)?

6. Do you believe that no one is righteous? How does the world respond to the message that all people have sinned against God?

7. Why will no one be justified by obeying the law? How are we justified? What does it mean to be justified?

8. How did sin impact Adam and Eve's relationship with God?

9. How and when did God reveal to you how passionate you were about disobeying God and living in sin?

10. What sin is hindering your relationship with God today? How can other brothers and sisters in Christ help you move towards living a life of holiness? What happens to the church's effectiveness in impacting the world when people aren't passionate about living a life of holiness?

11. How can we daily reflect that, through Jesus Christ, we have been forgiven of all of our sin? Do you have a hard time believing that some of your past sins are forgiven? What does scripture teach about this?

12. How can we hate our sin without hating ourselves?

13. How can a growing understanding of sin lead to a greater worship of God and greater love for the gospel?

MAKE IT PRACTICAL

14. Take a few minutes in your group and share with someone of the same sex a specific sin that you need prayer for. Pray for each other over the course of the week that God would help each of you turn from this sin and live in the grace found through Christ on the cross and Christ resurrected. Think of ways to encourage or support your prayer partner this week.

Study #3

Rescued by Christ: Part 1

Rescued by the Life of Christ

Read Luke 15:1–10.

1. Why does the shepherd go after the lost sheep and why does the woman go after her lost coin? What is Jesus teaching us about the character of God through these parables?

2. Why do we need to be rescued? What do we need to be rescued from?

3. What happens to our relationship with God and our view of the gospel if we overlook our need to be rescued and God's willingness to rescue us?

Read 1 Peter 2:21–25.

4. What stands out or challenges you from this passage?

5. How does the life of Jesus Christ serve as our model for how we should live? What specific characteristic of Christ is God trying to develop in your life? Do you have a passion for allowing God to make you more like Christ (the sanctification process)?

6. What is different between our lives and the life Jesus lived on earth? How does this allow him to be our perfect sacrifice and substitute punishment?

7. 1 Peter 2:22 says that *"He committed no sin."* What would have happened if Jesus didn't live a perfectly sinless life?

8. Why is Christ's perfect righteousness essential to the gospel? Why is it important to our justification?

9. When we put our faith in Christ, we not only put our faith in Him as the Son of God, we also place our faith in His perfectly righteous life, which, when we truly repent and believe, is counted as our perfectly righteous life. Why do we need Christ's righteousness to be counted as ours?

10. Can we be fully righteous outside of the work of Christ? What happens to people who are trying to earn their way to God based on their works and good behavior? How do we make sure we don't become such people?

11. How can you be grateful each day for the perfect obedience of Christ?

12. How can Christ's sinless life bring you into a deeper worship of Him?

MAKE IT PRACTICAL

13. Try to be perfect for a week. Really, try not to sin. But be honest with yourself and take a few notes on when you fall short whether it is impatience, anger, gossip, lust, etc. Use this experiment as a discussion starter next week to recap what we have learned about why we need Christ's perfect life to be counted as ours.

Rescued by Christ: Part 2

Rescued by the Death of Christ

1. At the center of the gospel is the cross. Why, at times, is the cross disturbing to focus on?

2. If we were to turn our backs on what Christ did for us on the cross, what would it do to our lives as Christians?

Read Isaiah 52:13–53:12.

3. List the characteristics about the coming Messiah Jesus found in this passage.

4. Why was Christ wounded? Why was He sent to the cross by God?

5. How does this scripture passage show that Jesus' work on the cross involved more than just physical pain? What else was Christ experiencing?

6. What was God the Father's involvement in the cross? What was our involvement in the cross?

7. Why do we seldom talk about or study the wrath of God?

8. How does the gospel deal with God's wrath? What does the gospel teach us about how our sin can be removed as an obstacle that keeps us from a restored relationship with God?

9. What is it about God's character that requires Him to punish sin?

10. How is the cross God's greatest display of love towards us?

11. What would living a "cross-centered" life look like to you?

12. How is the gospel impacting certain areas of your life such as your marriage, relationships, finances, your time, your ministry involvement, your career? What areas of your life are not being impacted by the gospel? How should the gospel impact these areas?

13. What would happen if an entire church were filled with people who were grateful for, in love with, and passionate about what Christ has done to rescue them from the wrath of God through our suffering Savior Jesus? What kind of impact would that have inside the church, and what kind of impact would it have on the surrounding community?

MAKE IT PRACTICAL

14. As a group, come up with a list of practical ways for making sure that you will never drift from the great truths of the gospel. Answer the question: How do we keep the gospel fresh, alive, and a fountain of joy in our lives? Review the conclusion "Never Grow Tired of the Gospel", and come up with some of your own ideas to add to the exercises suggested there.

Study #5

A Faithful Response

1. Why are faith in Christ and repentance of sin critical? What if someone has faith but no repentance? What if someone has repentance but not faith?

2. How would you define faith in Christ? How would you define repentance?

3. What happens when people try to make changes in their lives but never truly repent or place their faith in Christ?

Read Colossians 3:1–17.

4. Who has been raised with Christ? What does it mean to be raised with Christ? Can you be raised with Christ without faithfully responding to the gospel?

5. When we respond to the gospel, there should be a total life change. Paul points out that one of the changes will be to set out minds *"on things that are above, not on things that are on earth."* What is Paul trying to teach us? How should this teaching impact our lives?

6. Paul writes that we should "put to death" all of our sinful behavior. How do we put to death our sinful practices?

7. What sin is God currently asking you to put to death?

8. Paul also says that, as God's chosen people, we should do more than "put off" certain characteristics, we should also "put on" certain characteristics. Why is God passionate about our developing a holy and righteous character?

9. Do you think it is important for there to be a clear distinction between our behavior and the behavior of the world? Why or why not?

10. Examining the character qualities that Paul lists, which one will be the most challenging for you to live out?

11. How do all these characteristics exemplify Christ?

12. Paul writes that as followers of Christ you should be "singing psalms and hymns and spiritual songs, with thankfulness in your hearts to God" (v. 16). How is singing an outward expression of our love for God? Though you may be thankful for many different things, are you most thankful to God for the gospel?

MAKE IT PRACTICAL

13. If the proper response to the gospel is to put to death sin and put on righteous characteristics, what specific action steps will you make as a response? Share with each other what you are going to commit to doing and hold each other accountable to making these changes for God's glory.

Study #6

Advancing the Gospel

1. What fears do you have when it comes to sharing the gospel with others?

2. Is advancing the gospel something we should all be passionate about, or is it just for those who may have the gift of evangelism?

3. What should be our motivation for sharing the gospel with others?

Read 1 Corinthians 2:1–5.

4. Paul says that he went to the Corinthians with the message of the gospel. Are we committed to going to people, or do we wait for people to come to us? (Read Acts 1:8.)

5. Why is lofty speech and wisdom not needed when sharing the gospel? (Read Romans 1:16.) How do we often put more emphasis on our abilities rather than the power of God?

6. Paul writes, *"For I decided to know nothing among you except Jesus Christ and him crucified."* How should this verse shape the way you share the gospel?

7. What happens if our message is void of Christ crucified? Why is what Christ accomplished on the cross the crux of the gospel message and what we are called to bring to those who don't know Him?

8. Why is it so critical to be able to explain the basics of the gospel? What are some of the elements of the gospel that must be in our message when we share with others?

9. What does it say to you that even Paul had fears about sharing the message?

10. How does our weakness end up bringing more glory to God?

11. How can you rely on the Spirit and power of God to advance the gospel? What happens if we don't rely on God?

MAKE IT PRACTICAL

12. We need to pray that the people in our lives would be open to receiving the message of the gospel and that God will give us opportunities to share with them. Will you commit to praying for the people in your life? Will you commit to sharing the gospel with them when God gives you the opportunity? Write down the names of some of the people you want to reach with the gospel.

NOTES

Introduction

p. 15:   C. J. Mahaney, *Living the Cross Centered Life*. Colorado Springs, CO: Multnomah Publishing, 2006, 15.

Chapter 2: Holiness of God

p. 23:   A. W. Tozer, *The Knowledge of the Holy*. New York, N.Y: Harper and Row Publishing, 112.

Chapter 4: A Perfect Judge

p. 32:   J. I. Packer, *Knowing God*. Downers Grove, IL: InterVarsity Press, 1973, 146.

Chapter 7: Sin Enters the World

p. 46:   John Stott, *The Cross of Christ*. Downers Grove, IL: InterVarsity Press, 1986, 92.

Chapter 11: God's Wrath

p. 62:   Jerry Bridges, *The Gospel for Real Life*. Colorado Springs, CO: NavPress, 2002, 2003, 51.

Chapter 14: Christ Our Substitute

p. 76:   Mark Dever, *It is Well*. Wheaton, IL: Crossway, 2010, 56.

Chapter 15: Justified by Faith

p. 79:   Leon Morris, *The Atonement: Its Meaning & Significance*. Downers Grove, IL: InterVarsity Press, 1983, 193.

Chapter 16: The Great Trade

p. 84:   Wayne Grudem, *Systematic Theology*. Grand Rapids, Michigan: Zondervan, 1996, 574.

Chapter 17: Christ Our Ransom

p. 87:   Mark Dever, *It Is Well*. 72.

Chapter 21: Dwelling with God

p. 104:   John Piper, *God Is the Gospel*. Wheaton, IL: Crossway, 2005, 12.

Chapter 28: Mourning Sin

p. 133:   Martyn Lloyd Jones, *Studies in the Sermon on the Mount*. Grand Rapids, MI: Wm. B. Eerdmans, 1959, 47.

Chapter 33: Advancing the Gospel

p. 156:   Charles Spurgeon, *Soul Winner*. New Kingston, PA: Whitaker House Publishing, 1995, 157.

Chapter 37: Boasting in the Cross

p. 172:   Martyn Lloyd Jones, The Cross. Wheaton, IL: Crossway, 1986, 55.

Connect with the Author

If you would like to comment on the *Gospel Revolution*, share a story of how it has affected your life, ask a question, or discuss the gospel, I'd love to hear from you.

Facebook.com/GabrielStevenG

Email: gabrielsteven@yahoo.com

Other resources available from Home Improvement Ministries:

Parenting

Raising a Trailblazer, Virginia Friesen. (book)
Parenting by Design, Paul and Virginia Friesen.
    (DVD series, with study guide)
The Father's Heart, Paul and Virginia Friesen.
    (DVD series, with study guide)

Dating, Engagement

Letters to My Daughters, Paul Friesen. (book)
Before You Save the Date, Paul Friesen. (book)
So You Want to Marry My Daughter?, Paul Friesen. (book)
Engagement Matters, Paul and Virginia Friesen. (study guide)

Marriage

Restoring the Fallen, Earl and Sandy Wilson, Paul and Virginia
    Friesen, Larry and Nancy Paulson. (book)
In Our Image, Paul and Virginia Friesen. (study guide)
Jesus on Marriage, Paul and Virginia Friesen. (study guide)
Recapturing Eden, Paul and Virginia Friesen.
    (DVD series, with study guide)
Created in God's Image, Paul and Virginia Friesen.
    (DVD series, with study guide)

For more information about Home Improvement Ministries or to order
any of our products, please contact us:

Call: 781-275-6473

Email: info@himweb.org

Write: Home Improvement Ministries
    213 Burlington Road, Suite 101-B
    Bedford, MA 01730 USA

Online: www.HIMweb.org/books (for the online bookstore)
    www.HIMweb.org/speak (to book speakers)
    www.HIMweb.org/fb   (to reach us on Facebook)